Start
and run an
Internet
Business

Visit our How To website at www.howto.co.uk

At **www.howto.co.uk** you can engage in conversation with our authors – all of whom have 'been there and done that' in their specialist fields. You can get access to special offers and additional content but most importantly you will be able to engage with, and become a part of, a wide and growing community of people just like yourself.

At **www.howto.co.uk** you'll be able to talk and share tips with people who have similar interests and are facing similar challenges in their lives. People who, just like you, have the desire to change their lives for the better – be it through moving to a new country, starting a new business, growing your own vegetables, or writing a novel.

At **www.howto.co.uk** you'll find the support and encouragement you need to help make your aspirations a reality.

You can go direct to **www.start-and-run-an-internet-business.co.uk** which is part of the main How To site.

How To Books strives to present authentic, inspiring, practical information in their books. Now, when you buy a title from **How To Books**, you get even more than just words on a page.

Start
and run an
Internet
Business

Carol Anne Strange

howtobooks / **smallbusinessstart-ups**

Published by How To Books Ltd,
Spring Hill House, Spring Hill Road, Begbroke
Oxford OX5 1RX, United Kingdom.
Tel: (01865) 375794. Fax: (01865) 379162.
info@howtobooks.co.uk
www.howtobooks.co.uk

How To Books greatly reduce the carbon footprint of their books by sourcing
their typesetting and printing in the UK.

First published 2007
Second edition 2009

British Library Cataloguing in Publication Data.
A catalogue record for this book is available from the British Library.

ISBN 978 1 84528 356 8

Produced for How To Books by Deer Park Productions, Tavistock
Typeset by Kestrel Data, Exeter, Devon
Printed and bound by Cromwell Press Group, Trowbridge, Wiltshire

NOTE: The material contained in this book is set out in good faith for general
guidance and no liability can be accepted for loss or expense incurred as a result
of relying in particular circumstances on statements made in the book. Laws and
regulations are complex and liable to change, and readers should check the
current position with the relevant authorities before making personal
arrangements.

Contents

v

Acknowledgements

Special thanks to Mark Fenwick, my partner in life and business, for his support, belief and wisdom, and for his extraordinary ability to keep calm during the occasional technical crisis.

I wish to especially thank the inspirational Karl Moore for providing the book's foreword. Karl is a friend, fellow creator and a highly successful entrepreneur, who I've had the immense pleasure of working with online for several years.

I'd like to express my gratitude to the entrepreneurs who have contributed to this book, and to the publishing and editorial team at How To Books Ltd.

Thank you also to fellow cohorts Andrew Richardson, John Miller, Richard Strange and Philip N. Thompson, and all those who continue to inspire and be inspired by online entrepreneurship.

And, finally, thank you to you – the reader – for making this world a much more interesting and inspiring place as a result of your entrepreneurial vision.

About the Author

Carol Anne Strange has worked in the creative industries as a writer since 1985. She is author of many books, including best-selling ghost written titles, and her writing has been published throughout the world in print and electronic media. Although specialising in writing factual content, Carol is also an award-winning creative writer.

Previously, Carol has mentored writing students with the Writers Bureau. Over the years, she has also mentored and collaborated with writers, artists and film-makers. As a result of her experience in the creative industries, Carol became a partner in Red Arc Media – a provider of print and digital resources chiefly for writers, artists and photographers.

At the time of writing, Carol is engaged with several book commissions. She is also undertaking a MA Professional Writing degree after gaining a place at the University College Falmouth. Further information is available at www.carolannestrange.co.uk.

Preface

Welcome to the second edition of How to Start and Run an Internet Business. If you're thinking of starting a web-based venture – or have already dipped your toes into the entrepreneurial opportunities in cyberspace – you will find the new edition packed full of up-to-date guidance, suggestions, insights and inspiration to help you make a success of your internet business. But, first, let me share with you my own experience of making a profit from the web.

I first ventured online in the early 1990s. As a writer, I was excited at the potential of this vast information resource. I felt I had the world and all its knowledge at my finger-tips. As you can imagine, and what was probably the same for you when you first went online, I spent hour upon hour surfing the internet and became a digital information explorer. I deprived myself of sleep. It was so addictive. But what a fantastic resource for my writing career! At the same time, I discovered the wonders of email communication and also experienced the unbelievable frustration of technical issues, unexplained gremlins, computer hard-drive meltdowns and the horrors of computer viruses. Yet, when working effectively, the internet and all its associated digital benefits exceeded my expectations.

It didn't take me too long to explore the potential of online income generation opportunities. I had been self-employed for a long time as a freelance writer and any chance to improve my often precarious financial situation was to be grasped. I looked into and tried many different schemes to make a profit. Some worked albeit on a small scale and others fell by the wayside. What the internet did do though was provide greater opportunities in my writing business. Before long, I was gaining contracts to write for companies in America, Canada and Europe, as well as here in the UK, and by creating a website I generated more interest and gained other associated opportunities that I may never have found if it wasn't for being online.

Much later, on meeting Mark, my partner, we looked for further online opportunities that would allow us to live a more flexible lifestyle so we could concentrate on our creative goals. At the time, Mark was still relatively new to computers and the internet, but we worked together to create a variety of online opportunities and websites, while increasing our knowledge and web publishing skills. It was at times incredibly frustrating (still is occasionally when challenged with computer glitches) and we made mistakes along the way. But that's all part of experience. In the early years of the new millennium, beyond the aftermath of the dotcom meltdown, we began to experiment with a variety of online ventures, some of which proved profitable in a small but significant way. I gained a place at City University, London to undertake a post-graduate certificate in digital entrepreneurship and it was during this period that the foundations were made for several successful online ventures, including our writers' jobs and opportunities board, writethismoment.net.

To date we are still publishing online, offering a variety of services and constantly following up on new ideas, alongside our colleagues in cyberspace. Many of the opportunities we have created have grown organically on a low budget and continue to grow in value, allowing us to pursue our other life goals. The experience gained has proved a revelation, but I'm delighted to be able to share this experience and knowledge within the pages of this book in the hope that you . . . the budding internet entrepreneur . . . will find it beneficial in developing your own profitable web ventures.

Web venture ideas

◆ Looking for a business you can start online? Don't know what to focus on? Throughout the book you'll find short paragraphs under the title of **web venture ideas** which aim to give you some pointers, ideas and inspiration for finding your own web venture.

Foreword by Karl Moore

'Follow your bliss and doors will open where there were no doors before.'

Joseph Campbell

The internet is an opportunity waiting to happen.

For me, it started ten years ago – when the Web was in its infancy, and domains such as business.com had been snapped up for mere pennies just months before. I was earning £4,000 per year, working in the accounts section of a local electricity company. I left to start up online – and was branded a 'fool' for leaving that job-for-life.

A decade on, and I now own a network selling thousands of products, distributed over 200 websites. I command an army of 20,000 affiliates and run a handful of popular forum sites, and three different radio stations. Not only that, as I write, we're about to float on the stock market – as part of a nine-figure merger. And I still spend much of my time working in pyjamas, tapping away in my home office.

For me, this all 'just happened'. I followed my bliss – and got where I wanted to be. If you were to ask me the exact steps I took, I'm not sure I could give you an answer. But I know someone that could. Carol Anne Strange is not only a friend, but she has also provided sound business guidance over the past five years. We've written courses together. We've created marketing campaigns together. She's even written for my personal blog at www.karlblog.com – something I'm very particular about.

There's no doubt about it. Carol knows how people succeed in the online world. And inside this book, she's documented those precise steps – to help you reach your own potential in this online world.

The internet is still evolving. It has yet to reach its potential. Don't think you've missed the boat, or that there's nothing left of the pie. Your empire is just waiting to be built. And the only right time and right place – is right here, right now. Are you ready to take that leap with your own online business? This book is the best place to start.

Incidentally, the job-for-life electricity company closed down some seven years ago – making thousands redundant. It serves as a great reminder that extraordinary luck comes from taking extraordinary decisions.

To quote American mythologist Joseph Campbell once again: 'The cave you most fear to enter, holds the treasures you seek.'

I wish you the very best in seeking your own online treasure!

Karl Moore
www.karlmoore.com

1
Discover the Profitable Internet

If you would like to set up your own online business, you'll find plenty of opportunities. Chapter 1 explores the amazing and evolving medium that is the World Wide Web and looks at some of the success stories of recent times. You'll discover the advantages of starting an internet business and will be able to assess your entrepreneurial potential.

CREATING FORTUNES

With the steady growth of internet users around the world and quicker, safer and more reliable technology, the opportunity to set up and run a viable internet business from the comfort of your own home has never been easier. In fact, anyone has the potential to be an internet entrepreneur: you need to start with the right idea, passion, determination and internet access to set you on your way to success.

Since the dotcom crash in the late 1990s which ended in a stock market collapse and the fall of many venture capital funded online companies, the internet has been quietly evolving. Budding entrepreneurs, including some who managed to pick themselves up after the cataclysmic crash, have tentatively found their way forward – making sure that their businesses have a solid basis for income generation (unlike many of their predecessors).

Slowly but surely, the internet has matured and is bearing fruit. The timing has played a factor. With the advent of broadband technology, the internet is faster than ever before and user experience is far more reliable too. More of the world is online and, for most people, computers are a part of everyday life. It's also created mass changes in the way we shop and spend our money. The internet is now an established global community with information and business at the heart of it. People just about everywhere can shop, trade and find services online. Small, medium and large companies, from the sole trader to the multi-conglomerate, can have a presence on the web with their virtual shop windows open for business 24/7 every day of the year. This is good news for the digital entrepreneur looking to make their fortune online.

The internet's impact

The potential of the net is far-reaching and certainly has an impact within the business world at a multitude of levels. There are more budding online entrepreneurs than ever before, setting up small web-based businesses, trading in products or services from their spare rooms at home. This is increasing week by week, fuelled by the need to earn some extra income to pay for holidays or by the desire to escape the rat-race and be doing a more satisfying job. Being in control of your own destiny, working in your PJs and even earning while you're asleep, sounds idyllic and far-fetched . . . but it is possible. You just need to make sure that you create a viable online business and then attract and maintain a loyal customer base.

How much success you achieve is down to being in the right place at the right time in cyberspace. Whether you're running an evergreen business simply selling a product such as natural body care for a regular income, or you conceive the next big internet business hit which you sell for billions to one of the top ten internet companies, you'll realise that there is no easy path to success. Establishing a business online is hard work and reveals its own set of problems. You just need to make sure that you have covered as many possible outcomes as practical, but more of that later.

It could be said that the internet is one of the greatest inventions of our times. The web has made the world smaller and more accessible. It has its downsides too but, for many looking to make a living, it offers a chance to pan for gold. If you're very lucky you might find yourself with a small or even large goldmine.

ASSESS YOUR ENTREPRENEURIAL POTENTIAL

The ability to start and run a profitable online business requires much the same personal and professional qualities as are needed to run any business. A degree of entrepreneurial flair – being able to think 'outside the box' – may enable you to come up with a great idea potentially worth millions but, for most people, having entrepreneurial skills just to establish an online business, make it profitable and see it grow is the primary goal.

So do you possess what it takes to be an internet entrepreneur? Consider the following:

1. Do you find it easy to come up with new ideas?
2. Do you have a positive attitude?
3. Are you energetic and resilient?
4. Are you organised and meticulous?
5. Are you prepared to work all hours to make your venture successful?
6. Do you have the ability to think laterally, especially when solving problems?
7. Do you rise to challenges?
8. Does your enthusiasm inspire other people?
9. Are you willing to take calculated risks on something you are passionate about?
10. Can you visualise your success?

You should be able to answer a resounding 'yes' to all these self-assessment questions. If you have any doubts, these need to be addressed before you start out on the entrepreneurial path.

Entrepreneurs are people of all ages and from all backgrounds. There are no prerequisites in terms of qualifications, but it helps if you have a good idea and a burning passion to succeed.

There is a multitude of budding internet entrepreneurs vying to make their venture succeed. Many will fail because they don't possess the essential qualities that will push over the inevitable obstacles along the way. By careful self-assessment you can build on the qualities you have (more about turning your weaknesses into strengths in the next chapter) and have a better chance of achieving your dreams.

Whether your entrepreneurialism is fuelled by need – an example is that of Alex Tew, the million-dollar pixel entrepreneur who made his fortune by creating an innovative advertising website that would fund him through university – or whether you dream of achieving success because it's there to be seized, the potential can only be realised through hard work and the personal qualities that will drive you forward. If you have what it takes, the world really is at your fingertips on your computer keyboard.

 From the moment you decide to start up an internet business, develop a strong work ethic and disciplined routine. Be the successful entrepreneur that you wish to be.

ADVANTAGES OF SETTING UP AN INTERNET BUSINESS

According to Internet Statistics, 1,463,632,361 of the world's population were using the internet in June 2008. It is a figure that is set to grow with the continued proliferation of broadband and emerging technology. That's all good news for internet entrepreneurs looking to launch a business online.

In comparison with the traditional offline way of conducting business, the internet offers plenty of advantages:

◆ You can launch a web business on a low budget.

◆ A website offers a virtual 'shop window' accessible to the world.

◆ A website is potentially open for business 24/7, every day of the year.

◆ Possible reduced costs if you can run your web-based business from home.

◆ Efficient ways of targeting your market through web demographics.

◆ Multiple cost-effective ways of advertising your web venture.

◆ Quick and effective online transactions.

◆ Ability to stay in touch with your customers and offer loyalty incentives.

◆ Greater potential for growth.

Possible challenges

Of course, with every advantage you can expect a disadvantage. It's true that the internet undoubtedly has worldwide potential for any budding entrepreneur and you can understand why many are dazzled by the prospects, but there's more to it than launching a website and sitting back waiting for the world to come knocking at your door. Many processes need to come into play, from website branding to marketing and ensuring that you gain enough traffic on a daily basis to convert your web visitors into paying customers. We look at the finer details in later chapters, but it's worth considering some of the challenges that you may face in your quest to establish your business on the web.

◆ Tougher competition – your contemporaries in another country may be able to offer the same service for less money.

◆ Your website can be like a 'needle in a haystack' – unless you market and advertise consistently, you may as well be lost in cyberspace.

◆ Although technology has improved vastly in recent times there are still occasional gremlins. These can be problems on your own computer or issues with the hosting company or with the internet service provider. The state of 'down-time' is something you need to plan for.

◆ Internet security – or lack of it in some cases – continues to be a threat for many internet users. Although there have been vast improvements in some sectors, threats still exist and you need to ensure that you protect your assets and your customers from security breaches.

◆ Customers can be fickle. If a competing website comes along offering better prices, incentives or service, you can lose custom.

◆ Everything tends to happen much more quickly on the web and customers expect a speedy response. You need to be sure you can act quickly and deliver the services in record time.

◆ The web evolves so quickly that you need to stay abreast of developments if you don't want to be left behind. A successful internet entrepreneur stays one or several steps ahead of their rivals.

CAN YOU SPOT A WINNER?

As a budding internet entrepreneur, it helps if you have an instinct for an internet hit. A gut-feeling in business has carried many of today's multi-millionaires to success, as well as steered them away from failure. Instinct is something that we all possess, but this inner awareness can be finely tuned with the benefit of knowledge. So the more research you do into the winners and losers, the more chance you'll have of developing a successful online enterprise.

◆ Find out why websites such as boo.com and pets.com became casualties in the dotcom crash of the late 1990s.

◆ Analyse why companies such as Yahoo, eBay and Amazon survived.

◆ Consider why Friends Reunited, Skype, My Space and YouTube succeeded where others failed.

◆ Look at the micro-websites, many run by individuals from their homes, which generate smaller but consistent amounts of income on a regular basis.

Although some success is down to an element of luck and having the right idea at the right time, you will discover that the winners are those who have worked hard on their web strategy with total belief and have hit upon something that people want or need. The winners are those whose websites have income generation potential.

WHAT MAKES A PROFITABLE WEBSITE?

A commercially viable website is one that is based on a solid business model. It has to have a way of generating income and the potential to make a profit. When I say 'potential to make a profit' there are websites that have been making a loss, yet have been acquired for large sums of money simply because they have a vast membership base. One example is YouTube.com which was purchased in September 2006 for a reputed £883million. YouTube, although said to be making a loss because of the hosting and technology costs, had 73 million viewers a month and 100 million video downloads daily. This demonstrates that your website traffic is as important as the income it can potentially generate.

Of course, the likes of YouTube.com, MySpace.com and Skype are high profile success stories. They tend to be few and far between. What about the everyday internet entrepreneur, running a website with a view to establishing a profitable venture – one that can make a small but welcome fortune over the longer term for its owner? And how about the stay-at-home parent who is looking to make some extra cash from internet trading, or a youngster hoping to pay their way through university, or a couple hoping to escape the rat race to make an online living doing something they enjoy? Does the internet offer a chance for them to generate profit?

Creating the right elements

If you look closely you'll find many websites from all parts of the globe that are generating income for their founders. These are a real mix of websites and ventures from general to niche, some selling products, others offering services. There are people using sites such as eBay to trade, or elance.com to bid for work. Some will certainly be doing better than others. What you're likely to ascertain is that every idea on the planet has the potential to make a profit, given the right application. You'll also come to realise that one person's rubbish is another person's treasure . . . just take a look at some of the bizarre items that are selling on eBay!

Creating a profitable website is about giving your web visitors what they want. Your site has to be easy to navigate. Your customer service needs to be the best. Your marketing campaigns need to gain results. All the elements have to be in place. However, success as an internet entrepreneur effectively depends upon the experience, drive, energy, creativity and skills that you invest in your venture. So, although we started out asking what makes a profitable website, you may have already guessed the answer. It's you!

TYPES OF INTERNET BUSINESS

Commercial websites can effectively be divided into two types:

◆ business-to-consumer (B2C)

◆ business-to-business (B2B).

B2C

This is any website venture, from big name stores to independent, sole-trader run websites, that sell products and services aimed at the consumer. Think of Tesco.com; Debenhams.com; Directline.com, etc.

B2B

This is any website business providing a product or service, such as information, technical solutions, consultancy, software, etc to other businesses. Think of FT.com; Silicon.com; Oracle Corp, etc.

EXPLORING WAYS TO GENERATE INCOME

Basically, there are two ways of generating income from the internet. They are:

◆ selling a product

◆ selling a service.

There is no mystery to making money from an internet venture. There are innovative websites, but making money online is just the same as making money offline. In fact, a solid, successful web business that is making money draws upon the same criteria used by most successful offline businesses.

Products

You can generate income from being the manufacturer, wholesaler, retailer or agent of a product(s). Your website may be set up so that customers can buy directly from you online, or the site can simply be an advert for your physical shop on the high street. Your website can be specifically built for your venture or be a shop front on a bigger store such as eBay. You may hold stock or be an agent with no stock (more about this in Chapter 11). Whatever your product, from popular, everyday items to the more obscure, you can sell online and potentially make a profit with the right approach.

Services

The service industry on the internet is as diverse as selling products. Your website may promote your own expertise/skills and services. You can offer online consultancy, or your website can be an advert for offline services that you provide such as hairdressing or car mechanics. Service websites may include membership subscription sites where members pay to access specific information – online courses or jobs boards for example. Perhaps you're selling your skills as an artist, photographer, writer or editor. You can even find psychics who offer tarot card readings online!

Profiting from website user content

The latest generation of internet start-up companies is focusing on developing websites that allow visitors to share and create the website's content. Revenue can be generated from advertising or investor deals.

Companies that use their visitors' content include the following.

◆ Last.fm – founded by Felix Miller, Martin Stiksel and Richard Jones, the London-based web venture tracks musical tastes and provides customised radio stations, connects users and makes recommendations. The website existed off Google adverts, Amazon links and donations at the start. The company now has larger offices and a growing team of employees.

◆ Trustedplaces.com is a community networking site based around travel recommendations which are provided by the site's visitors.

◆ Handbag.co.uk – an online community with a discussion forum which visitors post to. Discussion topics cover a wide range such as beauty care, relationships, jobs and even dreams analysis. The forum members share advice and support.

◆ Ciao.co.uk – a multi-million-strong online community that critically reviews and rates millions of products and services for the benefit of other consumers. Ciao combines unbiased consumer reviews and up-to-date price information from hundreds of online merchants to make it the most comprehensive source of shopping intelligence on the web. It receives over 38 million visits every month, making it one of the largest shopping portals in Europe.

CONSIDERING OTHER INCOME GENERATORS

There are other income generators on the internet which are less easy to define. People are making very good money from including affiliate schemes or earn-per-click advert campaigns on their websites. Less certain and more risky is online trading on the stock markets. Some may consider this to be as unpredictable as online gambling, even though there are plenty hedging their bets and some professing to make a full-time income from it.

There are new business opportunities and schemes hitting the web every single moment, including the inevitable scams. We look at some of the viable opportunities, plus how to evaluate a business and how to find the best, profitable web ventures in forthcoming chapters. Suffice to say that business opportunities and ways of making money on the internet abound, but the most successful ventures often originate from the simplest ideas.

CREATING SUCCESSFUL INTERNET VENTURES

With the internet predicted to boom again or, at the very least, bloom, it is a great time to explore entrepreneurial ideas. The main change from the 1990s crash is that companies that are being acquired or proving to be a success independently today are real businesses with lots of customers and income generation potential. They are ventures that are offering products and services that people need. But there's more to it and, as you read through the book, you'll understand that there are many elements that make up a winning online business.

The most successful websites – whether big or small – are those that really shine in the vastness of cyberspace. They draw customers in like a beacon and tend to have the following qualities:

◆ Easy to navigate, fully-functional website.

◆ Products or services that the customer needs.

◆ Clear, easy-to-understand content.

◆ An effective website brand and design.

◆ Excellent customer service.

◆ Safe, secure and reliable site that customers can use with confidence.

◆ Loyalty schemes or special offers.

◆ Good and consistent marketing.

◆ Efficient customer communications.

We discuss more about what makes a good website in Chapter 3. To be sure, however, that your proposed website is a success, be guided by your own experience of visiting websites. Ensure that you run yours so that your customers are 100% happy.

MEETING SUCCESSFUL ENTREPRENEURS

Even if you're entirely satisfied to create a web venture that makes a small but welcome profit every month, it's still inspiring to hear about ordinary people who have taken a simple idea and created a website potentially worth millions or even billions. There are plenty of success stories to motivate you.

◆ eBay – founded in September 1995, eBay is The World's Online Marketplace®, enabling trade on a local, national and international basis. Launched in the UK in October 1999, eBay.co.uk has 14 million users and 233 million registered users worldwide.

- Friends Reunited – the website that started out to reunite old school friends was started by Steve and Julie Pankhurst and Jason Porter from a bedroom office in 1999. Friends Reunited was acquired by ITV for £120m.

- Million Dollar Home Page – student Alex Tew needed to find a way of paying his way through university and created a simple advertising page where businesses could buy web-space measured in pixels. Within five months, and through some clever marketing, Alex sold all the space and is reputed to have earned more than a million dollars.

- Mumsnet.com – this popular website was set up in January 2000 by Justine Roberts and Carrie Longton. It now has over 13 million visitors each month.

DISCOVER ENTREPRENEURS – JUST LIKE YOU!

There is a multitude of web companies launching every day by ordinary people with entrepreneurial vision. Many of these websites are in their infancy; some are quietly generating a modest income for their founders while others are growing at an extraordinary rate.

Take a look at the following internet entrepreneurs – people just like you – who have ventured online to follow their dreams:

Jon Robins – Meanandgreen.com

Jon worked in offices for big companies for many years. Then in 2004 he decided to escape the rat-race and buy a little run-down army surplus store that wasn't even on the web. Four years later and he has built a thriving online business that is now being run from separate offices and warehouse space. Jon's company buy in bulk from around the world and send out a huge quantity of parcels each week!

Tina Colquhoun – webinarwarehouse.com

The basic idea for Webinar Warehouse was to provide high-tech, interative webinars for translators, writers and freelancers on practical issues relating to their business and working from home. The founder, Tina Colquhoun, started out as a freelancer herself and had participated in a few of her clients' internal webinars that were designed mainly for product information. She believed that this area could be developed much further.

Advanced and intuitive technology is now readily available to everyone. Working from home is very much a 21st century option – comfortable, cost-effective and environmentally sound – and she wanted to promote this way of living and working, not least by taking advantage of the scalability of her idea. Tina hopes to go multi-lingual and expand to provide very country-specific webinars within their current fields.

Christine Lewandowski and Richard Evans –Singlewithkids.co.uk

Aimed at single parents, Chrissie and Richard's web venture singlewithkids.co.uk provides a valuable service for many parents who spend their evenings at home alone while the kids are in bed. The emphasis is on mixing cyber support with real life contact – and the online venture is working famously. Realising that cash is a problem for a large percentage of the UK's 1.9 million lone parents, they aim for low cost trips that bring a lot of single parents together (over 100 on a recent camping trip), and there are events all over the country every month. The club is funded by membership payments and also an online dating site and is growing rapidly in popularity due to a very large need.

Alison Berry – Idealpresent.co.uk

In 2004 with 10 years experience in the toy industry, Alison Berry launched idealpresent.co.uk – a free online gift advice service – to help people find the right presents for children aged 0–10. Alison's objective in setting up the business was to use her skills and experiences, whilst having a career which genuinely fitted around family life and looking after her own children. With a real gift for choosing presents that children loved, idealpresent.co.uk was born.

A few years on and idealpresent.co.uk offers a great service, advising what to buy for children, and where to buy it – from 10,000 ideas from over 200 retailers. The web venture continues with critical acclaim from the BBC. Their *Click* programme described idealpresent.co.uk as a 'great website'. The business model is one that provides an income stream with next to no overheads or running costs. A model that many other businesses could only dream of! As the largest publicly available database of toys and games in the UK, Alison is deservedly proud of the venture's success.

Paul Gunter and Andrew Shorten – BusinessMarketingBook.com

Friends and business partners Paul Gunter and Andrew Shorten have run their own web businesses (individually and combined) for several years, starting out when they were in their early 20s. With a passion for business and running ventures in internet marketing and domain name trading, they created an information product – domainprofitguide.com – which to date has generated over $50,000 in sales. Their web venture has been promoted using various internet marketing techniques, joint ventures with some of the UK's top internet marketers and from speaking at entrepreneur conventions. The inspiring partnership has since written a book about online and offline marketing for businesses, which was published early 2009.

Kate Haines – GreenFinder.co.uk

Kate Haines is an ex-teacher who decided to set up a green pages style website called GreenFinder after a lifelong interest in eco living. Interest in the environment has grown tremendously in the last few years so when GreenFinder launched in 2006, the venture developed rapidly. As a passionate environmentalist Kate was keen to use her skills to communicate sustainability and to help inform the public on living a green lifestyle. Kate features over 150 green business clients on the website and a green showcase stall which she takes to events. The website promotes everything green from cardboard coffins to eco wedding dresses and green cartoonists!

Elio Assuncao – Yodspica.com

Cardiff-based Yodspica.com specialises in information technology solutions and web design. The business was established by Elio Assuncao. Despite having excellent skills, Elio was at the time unemployed and decided to accept a Job Centre Plus incentive programme. He started Yodspica.com with no grant, no bank funding, no loans, no savings, and basically no money at all! Today, the company provides services in advanced web design, research, IT, multimedia, graphic design, engineering support, among others.

REFLECT UPON YOUR DOTCOM MASTER PLAN

If you're feeling inspired to become an internet entrepreneur, the next stage is to consider the type of website that you would like to start. You may already have a clear idea mapped out. If so you are part way to achieving your dreams. If you don't have any ideas at this stage, you may be able to draw upon your interests and experience to launch a website. The following may lead you to an idea.

◆ Do you have an interest or hobby that you can turn into a profitable website?

◆ Can you draw upon your existing skills, qualifications and experience?

◆ Do you have an existing business/service that you can establish online?

◆ Ask your friends for their opinions on what is lacking on the internet. It may spark a few ideas for solutions you could provide.

◆ Remember, many successful niche websites were established because their founders found it difficult to locate a service/product. Consider if you've had difficulties finding a service/product. If you have, chances are that other people have also had problems. You may hit upon a winning website idea.

◆ If you're thinking of setting up a website that already has plenty of established competition, consider what USP (unique selling point) you will offer to attract enough customers to your website.

◆ Learn to think laterally. Look beyond what is obvious to find innovative solutions to everyday problems.

◆ Study other dotcom success stories . . . can you improve on their ideas? Can you offer a different dimension to an already established website?

Remember – the simplest ideas often make the most profitable websites.

Once you have your idea, do keep it to yourself for the time being! Ideas are not copyright protected so if you share an idea with someone else there's nothing stopping them from stealing the idea and launching the website, unless they have signed a NDA (a non-disclosure agreement).

 Explore several established online business models. Ascertain what makes these websites successful. Now consider what you can do to make your web venture equally successful – if not better!

CHECKLIST

Have you:

◆ Considered what qualities are needed to be an entrepreneur?

◆ Looked at other websites to examine what makes them succeed or fail?

◆ Thought about the challenges you may face?

◆ Understood what is needed to create a profitable website?

◆ Reflected upon ideas for a website venture?

CASE STUDIES

Ian wants to turn his hobby into a profitable website

Ian enjoys cycling and is considering how he can turn his hobby into a profitable online venture. He has experience in the industry after managing a cycle shop for a number of years, and has many personal qualities and skills which he believes will contribute to his online success. Ian has researched existing cycling websites and believes he can create an information site that would appeal to cyclists worldwide. To gain profit from the website, he would be looking to sell cycling equipment and advertising space.

Maria is looking for extra online income

Maria has a talent for knitting one-off designer sweaters which she has sold on a local basis. She would like to promote and sell her exclusive knitwear online to bring in extra income for the family farm. Room has been set aside at the farm for Maria to run the business. She has started researching the market for her designs as well as reflecting upon what additional skills and equipment she needs to set up online.

2
Finding and Preparing to Start an Online Business

If you want to join the internet entrepreneur revolution and establish your own business online, you need to start with an idea or project. This chapter will guide you towards choosing an online business model. You will learn the value of research and reflection and start thinking about your business plan and goals for the future. Before the end of the chapter you should have thought through your project to provide a useful to-do list to take you through the stages of development, and have your mission statement and domain name in mind.

FIND ONLINE BUSINESSES THAT WORK

As you've gathered from Chapter 1, surf the internet and you'll soon find an eclectic and diverse range of successful web ventures, from multi-million dollar enterprises run by boards of directors to solo-owned ventures generating a modest but regular income and run by enterprising teenagers.

One interesting point you may glean from surfing the net is that these online businesses are incredibly varied. Some are based on sales of products and others provide a service. Some are extensions of offline businesses. There are even some that don't have any blatantly obvious way of making any money, yet have an enormous subscriber list or astronomical site traffic, which actually equates to serious income generation potential (remember YouTube.com and MySpace.com mentioned in the first chapter). Effectively, there are thousands upon thousands of online business models, ranging from the popular to the downright weird, making their owners a regular income or substantial money.

Believing in what you are doing

So what does this mean? It confirms that the internet is now embraced by millions who are confident to shop, trade or employ services online. It also confirms that it doesn't matter what you are trying to sell – providing there is a reasonable demand and you place your energy behind the project, you will make a success of your venture.

If you approach your web venture right you can sell absolutely anything – products, services or even thin air! It all starts with you and your belief in what you are doing.

Your success as a web entrepreneur is down to your authenticity. When you start a website that you are totally passionate about and believe in, success will follow. Any online business has the potential to work . . . even the most ludicrous ideas. It all depends on your ability to follow through and make it happen.

 When thinking about what internet business to start, take into consideration your life skills – interests, qualifications, previous jobs, knowledge and experience. Tap into the valuable resources that you already possess.

CONSIDER YOUR OPTIONS

Generating an income from the internet starts with finding a viable business idea. As is the case in the traditional offline business world, we have already established that there are effectively two ways of creating revenue from the internet:

◆ providing a service

◆ providing a product.

From surfing the web you will see that the internet offers endless possibilities for business to thrive and, depending upon whether you are selling a product or service, there are plenty of options to explore. You can:

- develop a new online business idea

- buy an existing online business

- expand an existing offline business

- trade online using established services such as eBay.

Let's look at these options in more detail.

DEVELOPING A NEW IDEA

True entrepreneurs are never short of ideas. If you see yourself as a modern-day Leonardo Da Vinci and are always coming up with new concepts, chances are that you will find an innovative web venture that you can develop from scratch.

Here are some tips for developing a new web venture idea.

1. Keep it simple! Great ideas are seldom complex in nature. Look at the previous big-hitter websites as a guide. Most of these are incredibly straightforward and their goal is to fulfil a need. eBay, for example, is basically an online auction house. Friends Reunited offers a service to help find and keep in touch with old school friends.
2. Think laterally. Look at what's already available on the web and see if you can find a new approach that is better for your potential customers.
3. Consider how you can take an old, established offline idea to transform into an innovative web venture.
4. Your success is down to numbers and how many people you can attract to your website on a regular basis. Social networking websites with a contemporary edge, such as MySpace.com, Facebook and YouTube.com, attract a massive amount of web traffic. Knowledge based sites such as About.com also command plenty of interest. What will attract people to your site?

BUY AN EXISTING ONLINE BUSINESS

If you don't want to develop a new web venture from scratch you could look at buying an established online business.

There are sites which advertise online businesses for sale. If you consider this route you need to do plenty of research and checks into any web venture that interests you before you financially commit yourself to making a purchase.

Ask the following questions.

1. How long has the website been established?
2. Are there records available of traffic statistics, membership, income and expenditure? Are certified accounts available?
3. Why are the owners selling the website?
4. Is the website in profit?
5. Is profit increasing from month to month?
6. Do you need to hold stock? If so, where can you obtain it from?
7. Does the business have long-term potential?
8. How quickly will you recoup the purchase fee?
9. What are you buying? Does it include web hosting, the domain name, site content and shopping cart?
10. Are any other partners involved or are you buying the business in its entirety?
11. What skills will you need to maintain the website?
12. Does the website have a good reputation?

Established web ventures can cost anything from a few hundred to many thousands of pounds. Sites that have a solid record for attracting large amounts of traffic, repeat custom or a good income will certainly be more expensive.

It's vital that you make the necessary checks to ensure that the web venture is genuine, so do seek advice before you part with your money!

EXPAND AN EXISTING OFFLINE BUSINESS

If you are already running a business offline, it may certainly be worth your while establishing an online presence either as a marketing tool or as a way of selling your products or services to a wider audience.

Over the past decade many of the major high street stores, in particular, have secured a web presence. Now you don't need to go to the supermarket to buy your weekly groceries. You can shop online in the comfort of your home from any of the big nationals such as Tesco.com, Iceland.com or Asda.com and have your food shopping delivered to your door. You can buy products for your home: computers, TVs, stationery and even motor accessories from stores that have a high street presence. However, smaller offline businesses too are finding that they can secure extra business and increase their income from having an online presence.

Some points to consider:

1. Will you use your online presence for marketing your offline venture, or do you intend to establish an online store where customers can buy products or services online?
2. Consider your catchment area. Can you sell your products or services locally, nationally or globally? Think about the logistics involved.
3. If you have a strong offline brand, make sure this is carried through to your website. Use your existing logos and trading slogans where possible.
4. Calculate how much time you will need to devote to maintaining the website. Will you be able to process extra orders in a timely fashion, or will you need to employ more staff to take care of fulfilment?
5. Recognise that the pace of business is very different on the internet. To stay ahead of the competition you need to be timely in your response to customer queries and ensure that your website is updated on a regular basis.

TRADE ONLINE USING ESTABLISHED SERVICES

If setting up a new website seems daunting, you could trade online using any of the established media.

Look at some of the options.

Selling products

◆ You can easily set up an eBay store shop front at a low cost.

◆ There are many services that provide ready-made store templates that you can use. Some can be customised slightly depending upon the package you choose.

Selling services

◆ If you offer a professional, technical, creative or secretarial service, set up a profile on a bid for work website such as elance.com. You can upload your CV and samples of your work for prospective clients to view and also bid for work without the need for your own website.

◆ Register with the main websites that cover your service industry. Make sure you have a profile or contact details listed on the main sites.

DRAW UPON YOUR INTERESTS AND EXPERIENCE

If you are entrepreneurial you may already be incubating the next big thing to hit the web! After all, internet success stories such as Friends Reunited started as a basic idea launched from home. Ideas aren't always free-flowing and although the thought of founding a multi-billion pound web company is appealing, most people, as we've already established, would be content to simply make a decent, regular living from their internet business.

The experience, skills, qualifications and interests that you have can point you in the right direction when it comes to choosing an online business. If you're passionate about something, whether it is reading, film, nature, horse-riding, cycling, art, music, gardening, fashion, etc, you will be more likely to make a success out of it if you can find a related service or product that you can offer.

Complete the following self-assessment and consider how your answers relate from a business viewpoint.

1. What interests/hobbies are you really passionate about? (Business ideas.)
2. How many people share your interests/hobbies? (Potential market.)
3. Can you identify a service/product that would appeal to people who share your interest/hobbies? (Market potential.)
4. What skills and experiences do you have? (Skills you can bring to your business.)
5. What associations do you belong to or can join? (Business associations and marketing.)
6. What skills are you prepared to learn to make your business a success? (Business potential.)

 You are more likely to work at a web venture that you're passionate about rather than one that rouses only vague interest. So, when choosing an online project, focus on the topics that excite you. Be authentic and true to yourself.

PLAN FOR INCOME GENERATION

As mentioned in the first chapter, some innovative and eclectic web ventures have failed dramatically, and many promising and venture capital funded websites either disappeared or side-shifted as the pressures mounted.

What is clear from the more successful websites that have survived and grown is that you need to have a plan for income generation – even if that plan is long-term. You also need to know how you will run your website in the meantime if income generation isn't immediately forthcoming. These points are fundamental to making a success of your venture.

As has been proven, popular websites that have maintained a web presence despite questionable profitability in the short term can go on to derive income in the long term purely from their popularity.

Web ventures that were established offline first are proving amongst the most successful because they continue to follow traditional ways of conducting business.

If you have been relatively successful with your business offline then you have a promising chance of making excellent progress with your web based business.

Many smaller website ventures are establishing a good online presence and a strong customer base because they have all the right ingredients (a business strategy) in place – and because they have formulated a plan for income generation.

Those web ventures that haven't documented a clear plan for generating income face certain meltdown once their seed funds diminish. So, if you haven't already considered your plan to generate income, now's the time to do it.

CHOOSING SERVICES OR PRODUCTS

Whether you offer products or services depends upon the business model you adopt. You may even offer a combination of products and services!

Here are some of the hottest products and services on the internet.

Popular products

◆ books

◆ consumables

◆ gifts

◆ gadgets

◆ software

◆ collectables

◆ niche products.

Popular services

◆ internet related services such as web design, web hosting, web marketing

◆ financial

- legal

- insurance

- creative services such as writing, illustration, art, photography, etc

- technical services such as editing, proof-reading, design, etc

- secretarial services

- consultancy.

To help you decide on the way forward, let's look at the pros and cons of selling products and services.

Advantages of selling products on the internet

- You can establish an informative virtual shop window for far less money than trading from a physical shop on the high street.

- Your shop is always open! Customers can shop at their leisure and buy products from you at any time.

- You don't necessarily have to hold any or much stock.

- If you have a garage or spare room you can keep any stock at home.

- If you are selling virtual products (e-books or software downloads) then your profit margins will be even more attractive!

- Overheads for selling products on the internet are lower.

- You have the potential of a national or international market.

Disadvantages of selling products on the internet

- Customers can't physically touch the product, see the quality or try it for size.

- Selling products such as clothing may yield a greater number of returns as customers can't try a garment in advance of purchase.

◆ Some products may be bulky, fragile or large and be expensive to deliver. This may raise the cost to the customer.

◆ Products may become damaged or lost in transit – you would need to consider this in your costs.

◆ If you find a popular product that everyone appears to be selling, you may find it difficult to be competitive on price.

Advantages of selling services on the internet

◆ You can draw upon existing skills, expertise and knowledge to provide an online service.

◆ A service which has an international appeal will provide you with a global audience.

◆ You can run an online service from home.

◆ Low start-up and running costs.

◆ Use your website to offer services online or to promote offline services.

◆ Customers often find online services more convenient and accessible.

◆ You can offer a variety of payment methods for online services.

Disadvantages of selling services on the internet

◆ There may be more competition, especially with popular services.

◆ Customers may prefer a face-to-face approach where some services are concerned.

TOP TIPS FOR CHOOSING PRODUCTS TO SELL ONLINE

1. If you are aiming to run a small web venture from home, choose a product that is easy to store, doesn't take up much space, and is lightweight and small for posting. For example: books, pens, socks, ties, crystals, jewellery, greetings

cards, ink cartridges, small craft items, hair accessories, watches, pet toys and accessories, CDs, card games.

2. Consider selling niche items . . . a collection of dog ornaments for dog lovers; quilting materials for quilters; art materials for artists; health books for the health-conscious; allergy-free cosmetics for people who have allergies, etc.

3. Can you use your existing skills to make original products? How about hand-made products such as knitwear, handbags, jewellery, greetings cards, sculptures, paintings, wood crafts, cushion covers, candles and so on? You may also be able to charge more for commissioned products and 'one-offs'.

4. Consider how you will obtain stock, how much you need and whether the price you pay will give you adequate profit margins.

5. Avoid buying large amounts of stock on unproven items or produce that may quickly become unfashionable or has a short 'sell-by' date.

6. If possible, check the quality of the products you buy from a wholesaler or manufacturer before you commit to buying in bulk.

7. Remember that some products may generate more returns, for example clothing, shoes, lingerie, electrical goods, gadgets or any product that could easily be broken during transit, such as glassware.

TOP TIPS FOR CHOOSING SERVICES TO SELL ONLINE

1. Choose a service industry that really interests you or you feel passionate about.

2. Draw upon existing skills, experience, qualifications or knowledge to provide a service wherever possible.

3. Consider developing a niche or specialist service that you can focus on, for example: a photographer who covers sports events; an artist who draws/ paints horses; an editing service specialising in academic books; a letting service specialising in rural retreats; a life coach offering consultancy to business owners, etc.

4. Consider the logistics of a service offered. Can you provide your services to a global market or do you need to operate closer to home?

5. Will you use your website to promote offline services, or purely online services or both?

6. Consider the market potential for your services. Do some research and look at your competitors on the web. Can you offer something that is better, more cost-effective or different?

7. Is your service seasonal or of interest all year round? Is there potential for growth? If so, can you manage this growth on your own or will you need help?

8. Think what your customers will gain from your services. Look for an angle or USP (unique selling point) which gives your service an edge.

HOW GOOD IS YOUR IDEA?

The great advantage about the internet is that it's a global marketplace and any idea has potential. However, if you want to know just how much potential your idea has, it's worth testing out the potential market. With an offline or localised business, this could involve undertaking extensive market research and conducting time-consuming surveys to ensure that your venture can attract enough custom. On the internet, however, you can access statistics with ease and virtually in an instant!

One way of doing this, and which has worked for several ventures that I've been involved with, is through analysing search engine terms, using your business idea's key word terms. Using a nifty programme, you can find out how many people have used the key words relating to your business idea in a given period. We look at this in more detail later as it's helpful for establishing a marketing strategy. Checking those search term key words now, though, will give you an idea of how many people online are searching for your product or service.

For more detailed market research there is a variety of online companies that can assess your target market and supply you with a variety of interesting figures. It must be said, however, that these figures are only hypothetical and your success really depends upon your ability to bring all the elements together to run a successful online venture.

RESEARCH AND REFLECTION ARE CRUCIAL TO YOUR SUCCESS

So, you have an idea for a web venture. You're eager to set up your website and launch your business to start making a profit. Before you jump in, take some time out for research and reflection. Doing this could save you time, trouble and money! It will also increase your chances of running a successful online business.

Research

Being knowledgeable about every aspect of your web venture will ensure that you are ready for anything.

Do the following:

◆ Research your idea thoroughly to ensure that it is viable. Do you offer something that your customers want or need? Are your prices competitive?

◆ Research your potential market. Who are your customers? Where are they based? How will you market your service to them?

◆ Research your finances. Do you know your profit margins? Do you know your costs? How much money do you need to make to break even?

◆ Research running a business. Seek advice from your business enterprise agency. Read as much as you can about setting up and running a business. Know your legal obligations. Be prepared for every eventuality.

◆ Research your competitors. How are you different from your competitors? What are your strengths and weaknesses? How can you make your venture better than the rest?

◆ Research technology. Will you create your own website or commission a web designer? What technology do you need to make your website work? How can you make sure your website is reliable and efficient?

◆ Research your venture's human resources requirements. Will you need to work with or commission other people (web designer, copywriter, marketing consultant, customer services staff, etc) to establish and run your web venture?

◆ Research growth potential. Is there potential for growth? Are you prepared for rapid growth? Where do you see your web venture in two, three, four or five years' time?

Reflection

Taking time to think through your ideas will work in your favour. Reflection is akin to tapping into the muse; it can give your venture a creative edge and help you come up with USPs (unique selling points) or an innovative angle.

Dedicate some time to reflection on a regular basis. Some entrepreneurs keep a note book or journal to record ideas or progress. This can be particularly beneficial, especially if you're working through a few challenges or issues that need a resolution.

To kick-start some active reflection on your business plans, try the following.

◆ Look at your basic business idea. Consider all the different approaches you could take with this venture. For example, say you are passionate about horse riding and want to start an equestrian website. Think about all the different angles you could take. Ideas may include a website to: advertise horses and ponies for sale; sell rosettes, tack or riding wear; offer jobs for people who want to work with horses; advertise a horse rug cleaning service; sell horse paintings or promote an online pony magazine, etc.

◆ What do you see yourself doing? How can you place your experience, skills and knowledge to good use in your proposed web venture?

◆ Reflect on your short, medium and long term plans. Where do you see yourself in four weeks, four months or four years?

◆ Put yourself in a potential customer's mind. What would you want to gain from this website? Does it have exactly what you're looking for?

◆ Mentally step through your plans to launch your web venture. What needs doing and when?

◆ Don't rush into decisions. Where possible, take time to think things through.

SWOT, SMART AND GROW

You'll soon discover that the internet and business world are full of clever acronyms. Three that you'll certainly find helpful are SWOT (strengths, weaknesses, opportunities and threats), SMART (specific, measurable, achievable, relevant and time related) and GROW (goal, reality, options and wrap-up). You could say that these are all academic, but let's consider how you might put them to beneficial use where your own web venture is concerned.

SWOT

You can use SWOT to effectively analyse yourself and your business ideas and goals. It's a reflection exercise commonly used in business and education.

A typical SWOT analysis might be used to weigh up your personal potential to run a business, or to analyse the potential of a particular business or product idea.

The following is a SWOT analysis to analyse the benefits of working collaboratively with a remote web business partner.

Strengths of working with a remote business partner:

◆ Ability to combine multi-disciplinary skills to develop the venture.

◆ Rapid collation, interpretation and implementation of information.

◆ Drawing upon shared knowledge, experience and resources.

◆ Encourages rapid development of project.

◆ Shared goals ensure motivation and mutual support.

◆ Brainstorming enables methodical analysis and evaluation.

◆ Flexible working.

Weaknesses of working with a remote business partner:

◆ Reliant on efficiency and reliability of communication between remote partners.

◆ Lack of clarity in email communication could give rise to ambiguity and mis-interpretation of information.

◆ Delays in email communication can date time-sensitive information.

Opportunities of working with a remote business partner:

◆ Potential to build strong, supportive working relationship.

◆ Encourages active learning.

◆ Ability to resolve problems through collaborative techniques.

◆ Ability to work remotely to reduce demands on time, finances and lifestyle.

◆ Potential to create a sustainable business.

Threats of working with a remote business partner:

◆ Issues adversely affecting technology or communication.

◆ Failure to organise and manage knowledge.

◆ Change in vision resulting in different outlooks.

◆ Conflicts caused by failure to comprehend digital dialogue.

By reflecting on these strengths, weaknesses, opportunities and threats, it is easier to make decisions of key importance and will also highlight areas that need more work to turn weaknesses into strengths, or give extra consideration to reduce threats.

GROW SMART!

These two acronyms relate to your goal-setting and can be used to plan tasks that you need to do to bring your website to fruition.

GROW means:

◆ Goal – identify your goal

◆ Reality – where you are at the moment

◆ Options – for achieving the goal

◆ Wrap-up – expected time to complete the goal.

SMART means:

◆ Specific – be precise and set clear goals.

◆ Measurable – provide a marker or chart to indicate when goals are being achieved.

◆ Achievable – make sure that your goals are realistic and achievable.

◆ Relevant – ensure that your goals are relevant to your mission statement or development plan.

◆ Time-related – set a motivating time scale to monitor your progress to achieving each goal.

You can use GROW and SMART on a daily or weekly basis to set goals for your business plans. It may help you to focus on a particular issue or task, thus making your project more manageable.

A typical goal for this week might concern planning your content for your website. An example of GROW would look something like this:

◆ Goal: prepare content plan for website.

◆ Reality: web structure ready for content to be added.

◆ Options: discuss content with partner to decide what to include.

◆ Wrap-up: start adding content within the week.

An example of SMART would be:

◆ Specific – to prepare a content plan for new website.

◆ Measurable – prepare the navigation menu and a listing of tier one and initial tier two pages.

◆ Achievable – I have decided upon the site mission statement and key words so I can start planning the content.

◆ Relevant – as soon as the first 20 pages of content are added, I can start introducing the income generation schemes.

◆ Time-related – the aim is to complete the content plan within the week.

If you find it easy to think things through, the SMART and GROW techniques may be extraneous to your needs. Use only if you find them beneficial in your planning.

START-UP CONSIDERATIONS

What do you need to start your web venture? Actually, very little! The great advantage of starting an online business is that your start-up costs should be relatively low compared with launching an offline venture.

All you really need to start are:

◆ a computer and software

◆ internet connection (preferably broadband).

Is that it? Well, a few extras might be needed depending upon the nature of your online business. If you're selling products, you may need to keep stock. If you're offering a service such as photography, you will obviously need camera equipment. It's also worth having a back-up facility so that you can regularly copy data in case your computer dies. Believe me, it does happen so don't forget to back up often!

Most successful internet entrepreneurs started their web businesses at home from their spare room or kitchen table, so you don't need dedicated premises. Obviously, if the business grows and you need to take on staff or carry larger amounts of stock, then you may need business premises at a later date. In the meantime, start small and keep your costs low.

TYPICAL RUNNING COSTS

It helps to draft a cash flow forecast to estimate your income and expenditure. Knowing your running costs will help you project what you need to do to break even or start making a profit.

Your running costs will again depend upon the nature of your venture, but are likely to include the following:

◆ Internet connection charge.

◆ Telephone charge.

◆ Web hosting fees.

◆ Online/offline advertising fees.

◆ Office consumables – paper, printer ink, pens, CDs, etc.

◆ Cost of electricity for your office (ask an accountant or your business adviser for current guidelines on the percentage you can claim against tax for running a home office).

◆ Professional fees (memberships to trade associations/accountancy fees).

◆ Insurance (you may need professional indemnity, public liability, or insurance to protect against loss of income).

WRITING A BUSINESS PLAN

If you require external finance to start your web venture you will need to draft a business plan. Many banks and business enterprise centres can advise you on how to prepare an effective business plan and cash flow forecast that will help you secure the funding you need. Even if you don't need to raise finance, it's still worthwhile writing a business plan or a business development plan to help you establish your mission statement (what you intend to do and achieve) and how you propose to run your venture. This will enable you to consider all the steps that need to be taken. You can also use a SWOT analysis on the business model, which will help you identify your venture's particular strengths, weaknesses, opportunities and threats.

Establish your short, medium and long term plans

Your business development plan should also include a projection of where you aim to be in the short, medium and long term. Think ahead constructively. Analyse your forecasted sales figures and this will give you a relatively clear idea of how you expect your business to grow over the projected periods. Allow for variations and also include ideas of what action you will implement if goals aren't reached.

No venture is fail-safe, but by visualising your plans and setting goals you have a greater chance of sticking to the plan and making a success of your business.

Web venture ideas

◆ Recently I was looking for an online store in the UK that focused on selling formal party/special occasion wear for children. Despite trying a variety of search terms, I wasn't able to find anything suitable. Of those I did come across, the range was limited and didn't appeal to my daughter, who was very disappointed with the lack of choice. It's possible that there aren't many online stores for children's formal wear because of the potential high returns of clothing that do not fit. There is still opportunity for offline ventures to show their range online though. I'm sure there are others like me looking for special occasion wear for children. If so, there may be potential here for a web business opportunity!

DRAFT YOUR MISSION STATEMENT

When you start formulating your business plan, one of the first things you should do is create your mission statement. This is effectively a condensed piece of writing, as little as a paragraph in length, that concisely explains what your website venture is about and its fundamental goals. It is exactly as the words imply, a statement of your mission, and will appear on your website.

It can be difficult encapsulating your website venture into a few sentences but, from a business plan point of view, it will help you focus on your goals.

Mission statement guidelines:

◆ Briefly introduce your company. It should objectively explain what you do, what you stand for and why you do it.

◆ Write a short paragraph – just a few sentences in total – relevant to your website's goals.

◆ This isn't a sales pitch so leave out any self-promotion to say how brilliant your website is (even if it truly is brilliant).

◆ You need to be totally behind your mission statement and believe it.

◆ Check out other company mission statements for examples of how other websites approach the task. Now write your own to suit your venture.

CHOOSING A DOMAIN NAME

If you're setting up a website one of the first things you need to do is choose a domain name. This is your URL (Uniform Resource Locator) which is your virtual address on the internet. Your domain name is what your potential customers will use to locate your website. Ideally, it needs to be a reasonably short, memorable name and you can be as creative as you like. Bear in mind, however, that a straightforward domain name such as www.photographyupdate.com not only gives a clue to what the site is about (photography), but is also useful in terms of search engine placement and optimisation. (More about that in Chapter 7.)

Domain names can be bought quite cheaply these days (see list in the Resource section) and have a variety of extensions such as .com (still the most popular); .co.uk (and other country variations which give an idea where the website is based); .biz and .tv are also available and other varieties are likely to come online in time. If possible, try to purchase the domain name with the .com extension and/or your country extension (co.uk/co.fr/co.za, etc).

Tips for choosing a domain name

Consider the following:

◆ Have several domain name choices in mind. Your first one might not be available.

◆ If possible, use a key word that relates to your product or service in the domain name.

◆ Choose a catchy, memorable name where possible.

◆ Make sure the domain name is easy to spell.

◆ Check the spelling of your domain name before you make your purchase. Once you've pressed the purchase button, you can't make any corrections.

◆ Remember to renew your domain name on time annually to maintain ownership.

When choosing the domain name, remember the acronym RAIL:

◆ R – recall. How easy is it to recall the name?

◆ A – aesthetics. How does the name look? Does it look good on business cards and company literature?

◆ I – impressions. First impressions are crucial. Does the name sound good?

◆ L – length. Domain names are limited to the 26 letters of the English alphabet, ten numerals and a hyphen – 37 characters in all. When picking a name, less is more. A short name is preferable to a long one.

PROJECT SCOPING

You can take your business idea further with project scoping. This involves breaking down the main planning elements of your proposed web venture into manageable sections for more contemplation and to give you a checklist of what needs to be achieved before you launch your web venture.

Initially you will need to:

◆ define mission statement

◆ identify roles involving any partnerships

◆ define brand

◆ consider design

◆ identify technical requirements

◆ identify information architecture

◆ define content requirements

◆ plan project schedule

◆ implement site development

◆ test through to launch.

Phase one – business planning

◆ Develop business plan

◆ Develop marketing plan

◆ Develop financial plan

◆ Develop management plan.

Phase two – project planning

◆ Devise project schedule

◆ Implement quality assurance plan

◆ Implement risk management plan

◆ Implement project development log.

Phase three – requirements development

◆ Confirm requirements analysis

◆ Confirm function analysis

◆ Implement design guidelines

◆ Identify user evaluation

◆ Confirm usability analysis.

Phase four – development

◆ Develop the site

◆ Implement beta (preliminary) testing

◆ Implement bug (any technical issues with the site) fixing.

Phase five – release

◆ Implement final testing

◆ Launch site.

Phase six – post release

◆ Monitor site

◆ Requirements analysis for continued development.

If all these terms, such as requirement analysis, risk assessment and so on, appear daunting, don't worry! We will look at these points and considerations in more depth through the following chapters.

In the meantime, use this project scoping as your main checklist to work through each stage of establishing your web venture.

CHECKLIST

◆ Have you decided upon a web venture idea?

◆ Have you researched the idea?

◆ What approach will you take to bring your venture online?

◆ Do you have a USP (unique selling point)?

◆ Have you prepared a business plan?

◆ Do you know your running costs?

◆ What are your short, medium and long term plans?

◆ Have you chosen and registered a domain name?

◆ Have you scoped your project?

CASE STUDIES

Mark has decided to open a specialist online book store

With a passion for art, Mark has decided to launch a website that will specialise in selling art books. He has developed a business plan and cash-flow forecast. He has some funds to buy initial stock and has identified several book wholesalers where he can purchase new and remaindered titles. He is currently considering a domain name for the business and his next step is to look at web design and hosting. He has set out clear plans for the short, medium and long term as follows.

Within six weeks

◆ *create the website and arrange web hosting*

◆ *order book stock and packaging materials*

◆ *test the website before its launch*

◆ *consider marketing and promotion*

◆ *launch the website at the end of the six-week period.*

Within six months

◆ *increase marketing and promotion*

◆ *review how well the business is doing*

◆ *look at ways to increase income*

◆ *review stock and choice of book titles*

◆ *consider which titles are best-sellers*

◆ *review website's content.*

After a year

◆ *assess the first year's accounts*

◆ *analyse the website's traffic statistics*

◆ *reflect on what products are popular*

◆ *look at selling off old or slow-moving stock*

◆ *consider introducing more customer loyalty schemes*

◆ *keep an eye on the competition*

◆ *check website's features and functionality*

◆ *conduct a survey with existing customers to see how improvements can be made.*

Sandra wants to offer a proof-reading service

After successfully completing a proof-reading course, Sandra wants to use her skills to offer proof-reading to businesses and publishers. This is an ideal service to offer online as it provides scope to sell the service nationally and even globally. Sandra has decided that she would like a professional looking website to promote her service and which allows clients to pay online. As clients can submit their material for proof-reading by email, Sandra is confident of providing a timely and professional service.

Although she doesn't need finance for the business, she has written a business plan. She believes this has enabled her to think through her business venture carefully, identify strengths, weaknesses, opportunities and threats and consider where she will be with the venture in a year's time. The project scoping has provided a useful to-do list for bringing the project to fruition.

3
Creating Your Website

Your website is your virtual shop window. It is the most important component of your web venture and it will either make you or break you! You can see why it's so important to get it right from the start and why internet entrepreneurs spend considerable time and expertise in ensuring that the site does what the customer wants. This chapter looks at what is required to create a successful website and provides valuable guidelines that will help you establish a website that's a winner with your customers!

DESIGN OPTIONS

Before you progress any further on your web venture, you need to make a decision. Are you going to design and create your website or will you commission a new media web designer to do the job?

DIY website

With improved technology and plenty of easy-to-use web building tools on the net, creating your own website is achievable, even for the most non-technical web entrepreneur! It's so easy that you could create a basic but professional looking website in just a few hours. That said, you may be limited with the use of templates and functions, but if you're using your website to promote a service or offline venture, then doing it yourself is a possibility and will obviously save you money.

DIY advantages:

◆ It's ideal if you just need a basic website to promote a service or offline venture.

◆ It's cost-effective . . . many web-building tools are free!

◆ You can update the site yourself at any time.

DIY disadvantages:

◆ You have a limited choice of website templates that are likely to be the same ones that other people use.

◆ You may not be able to include your brand colours.

◆ Functions and features are more limited.

◆ You may not be able to install a shopping cart or online payment system unless you have access to advanced features.

Commission a designer

By far the best solution for a serious website requiring such features as a virtual store, shopping cart and integrated online payment system is to commission the services of a qualified and experienced web or new media designer. This will ensure that your site is expertly designed and to the exact specifications that you need.

The initial cost of working with a web designer to create your site may be quite high and there is likely to be an annual maintenance charge. However, this may well be worthwhile if you want an original and attractive looking website that has been programmed from scratch, featuring your brand and all the site functions that you need.

Designer advantages:

◆ You will have an original website designed to your exact specifications.

◆ An experienced web designer will take care of all the technical issues that can arise when creating a website.

◆ You will be able to include full features such as a store front, shopping cart and online payment system.

◆ Your web designer may be able to provide additional services (probably at a cost) to help you market your website.

◆ The web designer will deal with any technical issues.

Designer disadvantages:

◆ A designed site will cost you more.

◆ Unless you have access to a CMS (content management system), you will have to wait for the designer to update your website.

◆ Unless the designer is working full-time for you, you'll have to wait for any technical issues to be dealt with in turn.

Try a partnership option

There is another option. If you don't have the technical skills required to engineer a fantastic, original website, but don't want to employ a web designer either, try offering a partnership share deal. For this to work you will need to have an income generation model in place for your website (so that the designer isn't working for nothing). You also need to find a web designer who is entrepreneurial and interested in such a partnership.

I have used this partnership option on a couple of web ventures and this has been particularly successful.

You would need to have an agreement in place which offers the designer a percentage of net income generated once the site starts to profit. Obviously, in the long term, and providing the web venture is successful, the designer could be in a lucrative position with a decent share of the takings. But that would also mean that you're in a lucrative position too. Consider your partnership as an effective working arrangement. Without the skills of your designer to establish and maintain the website you might not have the successful website that you have. Also, a designer with a greater vested interest in a web venture is more likely to go that extra mile in making the site attractive, reliable, workable and profit-generating.

THE ELEMENTS OF GOOD WEB DESIGN

The design of your website needs plenty of thought and planning if you want to get it right first time and create a strong and impressionable online presence. There are many factors to take into consideration. Good design isn't just about aesthetics; it's also about functionality and reliability. A website has to look appealing to attract your target market, but it needs to do all that it says it does . . . and more!

Internet visitors tend to be impatient and particularly choosy. If a website doesn't deliver quickly to their expectations, they simply move on. Web visitors don't have time to hang around when there is a whole world of websites to explore. Fail them once and you may also fail to win them back. They're more likely to find a more clued-up competitor who has the all-singing, all-dancing website that you should have had!

So, it's important to get the design and functionality right from the start. Of course, you can refresh the website at a later date with a brand new look and the addition of new features, but do test out the design with a focus group to gain honest feedback. That way, you can make the necessary tweaks and changes before you go live.

One thing to remember is that you will not please all of the people all of the time. The internet is such a big place, catering for a diverse range of tastes. As long as you follow some primary rules of good design, you'll have a better chance of pleasing most. And you'll find that being able to please most really counts for a lot!

Design elements to consider

Keep in mind the following points:

◆ Create an identifiable brand for your web venture.

◆ Be consistent with your page design. Use the same design and colour scheme for each page.

◆ Ensure content (text and/or graphics) is well placed on each page.

◆ Consider the style of your text fonts.

◆ Make sure there is a balance between text and white space. Do not make your pages look too cluttered.

◆ Provide a navigation bar on each page so that your visitors can always find their way round.

◆ Make sure your website is easy to use and reliable.

ESTABLISH YOUR BRAND

Your brand is what your customers will be able to identify you by. Developing your brand basically requires you to choose a colour scheme, logo and possibly a slogan (although not necessarily) that will help your business stand out in the market place.

Look at some of the major businesses – either on or offline – and you will see that they have a distinctive design brand that makes them identifiable. Walk down any high street and you'll soon pick out the major stores, banks and businesses simply by looking for their brand sign.

Creating your online brand

If you are an existing business with a brand identity it should be relatively easy to transfer your identity onto your website. If you don't have a brand then seriously consider creating one.

Tips for creating a brand:

◆ Make sure your brand design is distinctive.

◆ Be careful that you don't copy or clash with an existing brand.

◆ Your brand should be consistent on every page.

◆ Choose complementary colours for your brand and use throughout your website.

◆ Include your business logo . . . the top left of all your web pages is a good place to display your logo.

◆ Ensure that you use your brand identity offline too on all your business stationery and promotional items.

◆ If design isn't your strong point, work with a graphic designer or brand consultant to help you choose a winning identity for your business.

Your visitors will come to depend upon your brand identity once they have seen it a few times. This consistency is important in your marketing endeavours.

IS YOUR WEBSITE USER FRIENDLY?

Tantalising graphics, information rich content, fancy gimmicks and freebies are all very appealing to the web user, but unless your website is easy to navigate and use, you will fail to attract and retain your customers.

Usability is the key word. A fantastic-looking site with lots of interactive features and frills counts for nothing if the web user can't access your site, if links don't work or any featured services (such as chat, email, credit card facility or free downloads) fail to operate. As any e-commerce expert will affirm, it's great to have an original idea and to be able to sell it on the internet, but success largely depends upon the design of the website, its functionality and ease of use.

It is sad that of the millions of websites in existence, most fail to retain their visitors because of problems with usability. Even the professional, state-of-the-art websites belonging to major corporate bodies are not without their usability flaws. It would seem that the more complex your site, the more potential difficulties your visitor may encounter when trying to navigate it.

Think about websites that you have visited and have been disappointed with because of poor usability. What problems did you encounter?

Common usability problems:

◆ design errors

◆ poor navigation

◆ broken links

◆ pages that take forever to load (forever meaning anything longer than a few seconds!)

◆ features that do not work

◆ dysfunctional shopping cart

◆ a website that can't be used by people with disabilities.

To be successful you need to think 'usability' and have a site that is professionally designed, but easy for the customer to access at all levels. This is especially so for anyone who has diminished abilities. With usability legislation in force, aim to create a universal design for your website that is usable by all.

◆ Provide choices in the way features and functions are used.

◆ Eliminate unnecessary complexities.

◆ Allow the user to customise settings where practical.

Web venture ideas

◆ Do you have web design skills? Perhaps you could offer a niche web design service, targeting a specific industry. How about a web design service that focuses on creating websites for football teams, musicians, offline shops, garden centres, restaurants, hotels, holiday companies or hair salons? By focusing on a niche industry, you can target your marketing efforts so that it's cost effective.

REQUIREMENTS ANALYSIS

Before you start designing your website you may find it useful to prepare a **requirements analysis** to identify and define the design processes that require implementation.

Use the requirement analysis to orientate it towards a particular aspect of the design – perhaps the website's content, for example, so that you can plan out the action that is necessary to ensure that the content is effective in its delivery to the target user. Use the following as a template for your own requirement analysis.

Requirement analysis for the content of a website

The aim is to define the content required to meet the mission statement and drive traffic to the site, taking into account how the content will be delivered and managed. The goal is to evaluate the content to provide a set of markers to ensure the effectiveness of the content in capturing and retaining the target users of the site.

Analysing the content requirements for your website

1. **Identify target users.** Determine who will visit your website.

2. **Define mission statement.** Identify points of the mission statement and create content that reflects the users' needs.

3. **Identify user requirements.** Determine the user needs and target usability requirements.

4. **Identify content for search engine optimisation.** Conduct a key word search to identify content that will drive traffic. Identify key words with high profitability.

5. **Identify required infrastructure.** Establish a site content map (a linkable list to all the content on your website) to define the architecture of the site.

6. **Identify design requirements.** Determine how the content will be delivered and what technology, systems and software need to be created and maintained. Establish design of the site to carry the brand, taking into consideration the look, choice of text styles, use of images and layout for ease of use. Determine the system boundaries and logistical issues.

7. **Prepare content plan.** Identify the main navigation menu and subsidiary menus. Determine content requirements for home page and tier pages. Assess how the content will encourage users to purchase membership subscriptions/products or services.

8. **Develop content.** Draft content taking into account the effectiveness of micro content and main content in captivating the user, retaining the user and driving traffic from search engines.

9. **Evaluate content.** Check content for style, grammar, consistency and delivery. Ensure content is credible and written to encourage loyalty, trust, interaction and use of site resources and income generation schemes. Analyse content for usability. Use the evaluation results to improve the content for greater ROI (return on investment).

10. **Analyse design infrastructure.** Examine the systems and software implemented to deliver the content for any conflicts, weaknesses or discrepancies. Evaluate effectiveness of the design infrastructure and architecture for ease of navigation and user experience. Evaluate usability through focus discussion groups and user tests.

Like the project scoping, a requirements analysis is a useful document to have as it will help you conclude what you need. It is certainly beneficial for use when planning your website.

Develop a content management plan

Your next course of action is to establish how content will be developed and the processes needed to be implemented to manage the content. Determine any limitations for the management and storage of content and consider a longer term solution for storage of archive material.

 Look at your competitors' websites. Consider how you can make your website significantly better in terms of content and usability. Analyse first and then decide upon a plan of action.

PREPARE YOUR WEBSITE CONTENT MAP

Whether you are creating the website yourself or commissioning a web designer, do prepare a website content map to sketch out your proposed content for the whole site.

Points to consider at this stage include:

◆ How many pages will you need?

◆ What are the titles of each page?

◆ If you require multiple-tier pages, how will your visitors navigate these pages without losing their way?

Typical content areas may include the following pages:

◆ home page

◆ about us

◆ registration/log-in

◆ service/shopping pages

◆ news

◆ testimonials

◆ special offers

◆ contact.

These page titles are generic and you will obviously need to personalise them to suit your website's requirements.

Consider the following.

◆ Do you need a members-only area? Some parts of your site may need to be password protected to enable only membership access.

◆ Do you need a discussion forum? These are popular for membership sites or stand-alone sites where the web venture is actually a discussion forum – think ukbusinessforums.co.uk as an example.

Let's break down some of the main pages and consider the features you may have on each.

Home page

This page is where your visitors will enter the site. It usually contains the following features:

◆ The name of your website.

◆ Introduction – usually a couple of paragraphs to explain what you do.

◆ Navigation bar with links to all your main pages.

◆ Registration/log-in box.

◆ Search bar – useful for searching the site or searching the web.

◆ Testimonials – two or three short testimonials from your customers can prove beneficial.

◆ Advertising – this is the main page to include some small, relevant adverts if applicable to your site's objectives.

◆ Small print – links to your terms and conditions, FAQs (frequently asked questions), privacy information and copyright notice are usually at the foot of your home page.

There are lots of free features you can add to your home page including:

◆ today's date

◆ news feeds

◆ quotes of the day

◆ visitor counter (although these appear to be going out of fashion).

Do a search for 'free web page content' and you'll find lots of interesting features that you could use. Do not over-clutter your home page though. White space is recommended so as not to overwhelm your visitors. The keep it simple rule applies. Only include what is relevant to your target audience.

About us page

A few short paragraphs are usually enough for the about us page. Keep the information relevant to your website. If you don't want to give too many personal details, that's fine. Just provide some background information about the business, emphasising any relevant expertise, accolades and strengths. Keep in mind though that a personal approach, with some brief background information and even a photo of yourself or team, can inspire confidence amongst your visitors by showing the face behind the website.

Registration page

If you need a registration page for customers to subscribe to a service or an e-newsletter, keep the page simple and straightforward. Make sure you clearly highlight the benefits of joining. Don't ask too many questions in the registration process. Customers are often put off from completing any lengthy forms that ask for too many personal details, so make it quick and easy to register so they don't lose interest.

Service/shopping pages

This is the main part of your website that needs to do the work in selling your products or services. Include only relevant information. Keep product/service descriptions detailed but concise. You may need to implement shopping cart technology on these pages to allow visitors to make a purchase.

News page

You may want to include news updates through RSS feeds (Really Simple Syndication which are web feeds updated frequently) or a blog (an online journal) to your website. This not only helps drive traffic to your site through search engines (providing these news pages allow public access), but it also keeps your customers up to date. If you include an interesting blog, you may find that your customers will visit regularly to read your posts.

Testimonial pages

If you can gather positive feedback from your customers and gain their permission to publish their endorsements or testimonials on your website, this will certainly help your web venture. Good feedback will inspire new customers to trust in your product/service and it's worth devoting a page for any testimonials that you receive.

Special offer/freebie page

Everyone likes a special offer or, better still, a freebie. Perhaps you can provide a discount on a first purchase or sell off older stock at lower prices. Where freebies are concerned, consider if you can give away an e-book or web graphics or anything that your visitors can download free. If you have created the freebie for download yourself then this won't have a physical cost to you!

Contacts page

Your contact information needs to be on your website. If you are a small web operation running from home and do not wish to advertise your home address, consider using either a PO box number or a mailing address service. If you do not have resources to take telephone enquiries, then do make sure that your customers can email you. The laws are changing all the time as the internet evolves and there is greater insistence that online ventures include full contact information on their websites.

Some tips for designing your website

Consider the following:

◆ Be creative and start planning your website offline on a blank sheet of paper.

◆ Take your time! Think about the site's theme, look and style and how it will suit your target audience.

◆ Note where you want to place your web venture's name and logo.

◆ Consider how you will lay out your content. Will it be split into two or three columns? Will visitors have to scroll down the page to read content?

◆ Think about your site's navigation at this point and your multi-tier pages.

◆ Think about your site's dimensions and ensure that you cater for all web browsers.

◆ Don't over-complicate your website. The best sites tend to be simple in their design.

◆ Choose images and banners that are consistent with your site's look.

◆ Make sure links are obvious and in keeping with the site design.

◆ Make sure link pages open in a separate window so that visitors are not taken away from your website.

◆ Where possible and with permission, include full names and website links with any published testimonials.

◆ Avoid heavy graphic-laden intro pages that take ages to load into a web browser. Your visitors want to access your website quickly.

◆ Remember that the more pages you have on your website, the more complex your site, the more potential there is for things to go wrong. Make regular checks to ensure your site is fully functional!

THE IMPORTANCE OF WEB CONTENT

The internet's primary function is to provide access to information on a global basis. As a valuable commodity, information is what most web visitors seek above anything else. For the website venture proprietor, providing information-rich content and presenting it in a way that retains visitors should be a priority to establish a successful enterprise.

Despite the importance of content and the way it is presented, many websites fail to deliver. Here are some of the major textual content pitfalls.

◆ Content that is poorly written.

◆ Content that is sparse and uninformative.

◆ Content that is verbose and loses the reader.

◆ Content that is factually inaccurate.

◆ Poor presentation – use of font style or colour that is difficult to read.

◆ Inappropriate use of words: writing that is offensive.

◆ Use of localised terms, slang or colloquialisms that international visitors may not understand.

◆ Spelling mistakes.

◆ Poor grammar.

View a random selection of websites and take note of the information provided and the way it is delivered. You'll soon establish what works and what doesn't.

Armed with this research, you can start thinking about your own site and what you need to do to enhance your content.

Create clear, information-rich web copy

No matter what type of web venture you are involved with, it is essential to ensure that your content effectively conveys your information to promote your product/ service and is specific to your target audience. Whether you prepare the content yourself or have it specially written by experts, you need to consider the following salient points.

◆ **Be informative.** Give your target audience all the information they require. Make sure the content is detailed but concise. Make every word count!

◆ **Be accurate.** Your content needs to be precise. If the information you provide is vital to your credibility and reputation, make sure it is thoroughly checked for accuracy.

- **Be objective.** Make sure content is free of bias. You need to provide information that is objective.

- **Use plain English**. Avoid using slang or colloquial words or terms that an international audience may not understand. Write clearly, using plain English.

- **Update regularly.** Be sure to keep your information current. Check content regularly and make any necessary changes and additions.

- **Keep a balance.** The World Wide Web is the information superhighway, but it is also a medium for trading. Keep a balance between the two so that your content is informative and appealing, but also has the necessary pitch that will lead to you gaining the required custom.

Writing rich key-word content

Not only does your web copy need to be well-written and informative, it should also be delivered to optimise your search engine placement. We look at this in more detail when we cover search engine marketing later on, but you need to be aware of this in the design stages when contemplating your content.

Your web content has a crucial role in deciding your place in search engine results for relevant key word phrases (the words that your potential customers will search for) so it's important that you consider writing key-word rich content. You need to have the balance just right though. Too few keywords and your site will not gain the required exposure. Too many keywords and your site will be ignored by your visitors and search engine spiders (also known as crawlers which are the devices in place to check websites for inclusion in search engines).

Good web copy writing ensures the right balance of key word density, using the optimal number of search terms in relation to the total number of words.

Don't overdo the keywords though to the point where your copy becomes dull, repetitive, unappealing or reads like exaggerated sales copy. Remember to write with your target audience in mind. After all, it is your customers who will decide whether to buy your product or service.

All your key words should also be placed in the meta tags of the website code (check with your designer or design program). However, it is thought that with enhanced search engine technology, it's not as important to do this. It's what is on your website for public viewing that matters and gets you rated in the search engines.

Basic rules about writing web copy

Consider the following points:

◆ Always write for your target audience. Make sure that you give the readers what they need.

◆ What is the purpose of your web copy? What message are you trying to convey? Be clear with your objectives. Keep it relevant and don't go off on a tangent.

◆ Write most of your copy using the 'inverted pyramid' style. This involves writing the key information at the beginning of the article. It has the effect of grabbing the reader's attention and providing them with the important details from the start. Newspapers use the inverted pyramid style of writing successfully and this form of journalism is suitable for electronic publishing.

◆ Keep your articles brief and specific to the heading.

◆ Insert short sub-headings at least with every page scroll to break up the text. Make it easy to scan.

◆ Use short, captivating headings which are also key-word rich.

◆ Keep paragraphs and sentences short.

◆ Make every word count!

◆ Avoid use of slang or colloquial terms.

◆ Write for an international audience.

◆ Use plain English.

◆ Check that your grammar and punctuation are correct.

◆ Check your copy to avoid typos and spelling mistakes.

- Be brief in your delivery, but write in an appealing and informative style.

- Work to a maximum of 600-700 words per article.

- Turn your web copy into benefits. Inform your visitors.

- Check your copy to avoid ambiguity.

- Use bullet points to break up large chunks of writing.

- Edit your copy to avoid any repetition, verbosity or extraneous words.

- Only use underlining for hyperlinks.

CONTENT PRESENTATION

Your web copy needs to be presented in a way that is visibly pleasing and easy on the eye. Reading from a screen is 25% slower than reading from a paper publication and up to 75% of web users prefer to scan information on web pages instead of reading word for word.

Apart from the basic rules of web content writing, consider these points to ensure effective content presentation.

- Break up text, organising it into a logical sequence so that it is in manageable, bite-sized chunks to enable the visitor to easily scan the copy. Think of the FAQs (frequently asked questions) pages that appear on many sites. Here, the information is presented under relevant headings and sub-headings so that the visitor can abstract the details they require. Use short, bold headings and sub-headings. Use bullet lists to break up text and highlight important points. As a general rule, use one paragraph per point so that the reader can scan through the text.

- Highlight key words and links. Don't, however, use too many as they can distract the reader.

◆ The physical layout of your text on your web pages is all important. Make sure there is white space (clear space between text and other content) and that your text isn't too cluttered. Consider the text alignment on the page and avoid placing text so that the reader has to scroll both sideways and downwards.

◆ Watch out for colour usage. For example, yellow text on a white background is stressful on the eyes. Black text on white, cream or pastel background is still considered the best.

◆ Choose a clear font. Verdana or Arial are widely used for websites. Avoid any flamboyant font styles which are difficult to read.

If you take care how you present the information on your website, you will create an easy and attractive reading experience for your visitors. That means you have a greater chance of those visitors returning.

Where to gain web copy

You basically have three options for gaining content for your website.

1. **Write it yourself!** If you write well, have a good standard of grammar and the relevant expertise, you can produce your own content for your website. This is the ideal solution for a small site with a low budget or for one that doesn't require extensive content. However, check the copy carefully to ensure there are no spelling or grammatical mistakes.

◆ Pros – it's free and you can write original copy. You will own the copyright on the material you have written.
◆ Cons – if your writing or grammar aren't very good, it will show. Poor writing will spoil your website and make it appear unprofessional.

2. **Gain free copy!** There are plenty of websites offering free articles on a range of topics which you can use on your website. Conduct a search for 'free content' or 'free articles' and check out the resource section for ideas.

◆ Pros – you gain free content written by experts in their fields.

◆ Cons – the same articles are likely to appear on hundreds of different websites so you don't have any exclusivity. There may be restrictions on how you use the content.

3. **Buy original content.** By far the best approach is to buy your web copy. Information-rich websites and medium to large online ventures need good, accurate, well-written content to set them apart from their competitors. Engaging the services of a writer, preferably one who specialises in your content area, will enable you to gain original material to suit your target audience.

◆ Pros – you gain original web copy/content written by professionals. You may be able to negotiate the rights and use of the material on your website.

◆ Cons – you will have to pay for the material.

USING IMAGES ON YOUR WEBSITE

If the internet was purely text based, our visits to websites would be incredibly boring. The use of images, whether static or moving, brings another dimension to the web experience. Images, used correctly, can make a website appealing. They are also extremely important if you're selling a product or service that requires a photographic visual sample for the potential customer to appreciate. For example, you couldn't sell your range of jewellery or fashionable accessories if you didn't have clear images of your product to show your customers. No matter how good your text, some websites need images to secure a sale.

Consider the following pointers:

◆ Displaying relevant images that complement your web copy will attract your visitors' attention and make your website appealing.

◆ Avoid using large graphics on your website. Use small images and have an option to magnify the image or open a larger one in a separate box.

◆ Make sure images are sized correctly with the correct height and width to avoid distortion. Most web images should be around 72 dpi and saved as JPEG (for full colour images) or GIF (for more solid colour or fewer colour use images), format.

◆ If you intend to include multiple images on one web page, keep the total file size below 50K. Use photo editing software to size your images correctly. (Pixels should be around 72 dpi per image.)

◆ Label each image on your website with a title, caption or description.

◆ Use text links as a way of viewing or downloading images.

◆ Avoid intellectual property theft. Make sure there is a copyright notice across any larger images that could be reproduced to avoid people downloading them and using inappropriately.

◆ If your site is image intensive, provide a thumbnail view of each image so that visitors can quickly scan the images and choose ones they would like to see in a larger format.

◆ Make sure your images are effectively composed with a clear resolution. If they are illustrating a product, they should give a clear and accurate representation. If they don't, you need to mention this on the site. For example, the colours you see on web pages might not match the exact colour of your product so be aware of this.

Ideally, if images are important in selling your product, it's worth commissioning a professional photographer to produce the images that you need. You will be provided with a collection of photographs that are well composed and of a high standard. If you have a digital camera though, and are confident of your ability to take good photographs, it's worth experimenting to see if you are able to capture the quality images that you require.

Artwork and logos

If you're developing a brand so that in your web venture it stands out and is recognisable, consider your choice of artwork to make sure it suits the overall look and theme. You may wish to work with an artist to create a logo or artwork for your site. Some web designers offer logo or artwork creation as part of their service.

Words and pictures usage

It's important to note that you must not copy text or images from other sources (print, web or any published material) to use on your website without gaining permission from the originator. To do so could result in expensive legal action against you so do take care. We will cover copyright in more detail in Chapter 5.

 You have about 20 seconds to capture the attention of your potential customers. If your home page and content don't impress your visitors, or they can't find the information they expected, it's unlikely they will stick around or come back. Always design a website with your visitors firmly in mind.

CHECKLIST

◆ Have you drafted a requirements analysis and a content plan for your website?

◆ Have you decided on your website's brand, theme and look?

◆ Have you made a decision on who will design your site?

◆ Do you know how you will obtain your images and copy?

◆ Do you know what features will appear on your website?

◆ Have you designed your website to be user-friendly?

CASE STUDIES

Ismail has created a science fiction fan website

Ismail decided to work with a web designer to create a site that has interactive features to appeal to his visitors, as well as a dedicated members' only area. One of the focal points of the site is the discussion board where members meet to discuss and review films and books. Ismail felt it was important to have a strong brand image to differentiate it from other fan sites.

Charlotte wants to promote her local wedding make-up service online

After running a wedding make up service locally for a number of years, Charlotte wants to create a website to promote her service, as well as provide advice on make-up and beauty. She is hoping to gain some income from her website from affiliates and running relevant pay-per-click advertising. She only needs a basic website with about 12 pages of content, and decided to approach a trainee web designer at a local college to build the website for her. She has a CMS (content management system) which allows her to update the website herself.

4
Preparing to Go Online

The reliability of the technology you choose is crucial to your web venture's success. This chapter explores what it takes to bring a website online. Find out about shopping carts and online payment systems. Learn how to keep your website and computer secure and what you can do to avoid downtime.

CHOOSING TECHNOLOGY

Choosing technology can be a daunting prospect for any company establishing their presence in the global market place. Many companies spent millions on their computer technology before the dotcom bust of the late '90s. They invested in the latest developments in an effort to keep ahead in the worldwide market place. Since then, many online ventures are understandably cautious as they build their empires. Gone is the complacency where spending is concerned. Now, low-cost launches are considered the way forward. Companies, big or small, have to contend with budget constraints and choose their technology, web design and hosting solutions with care.

Of course, it's easy to be seduced by the latest software, gadgets and web solutions. Technology changes so quickly that new versions of operating systems and upgraded software are launched before you've had your money's worth out of last year's products. What you need to do to keep a hold of your precious budget is to assess your technology requirements and only purchase what you need, focusing on how it would benefit your site's visitors.

Establish your requirements

Before you make a decision on what technology to use, consider your company's technology requirements (conduct a technology requirements analysis using the same approach we covered earlier) and the factors that will enable you to achieve your website's objectives.

◆ Make a priority list of the basic technology you will need to deliver your website. Apart from the hardware, keep in mind software, design and hosting requirements.

◆ Only use the technology that will meet your customers' needs.

◆ Think about your network and data storage capacity and how this will grow.

◆ Plan ahead for at least several years and make sure that the technology you choose provides flexibility for upgrades rather than becoming obsolete.

◆ Engage technology that works efficiently. The service should be reliable, relatively fast and adaptable enough to accommodate change and expansion as the company evolves.

◆ Choose simplicity over complexity. More often than not, the simpler the technology, the fewer problems you will have. Your technology doesn't need to be cutting-edge. What's important is that it does the job effectively so that you have a satisfied customer as a result.

KEEPING TECHNOLOGY COSTS LOW

In recent years, some areas of technology have reduced in price. This is especially the case where data storage and network applications are concerned.

You can reduce your technology spend further by implementing the following:

◆ Don't purchase tools or gadgets unless they are vital to your venture's success and are going to be used on a regular basis.

◆ Plan ahead to prepare for your website's growth. Many tend to buy too much server capacity before they need it.

◆ Consider your hardware requirements. Do you really need to buy the most expensive computer in the store? A more basic, cost-effective model is likely to provide you with all that you need.

◆ Look for special deals on hardware purchases, but do your homework to make sure that you really are gaining the best deal.

◆ Negotiate software packages when you choose hardware. If you're buying software direct from a software manufacturer such as Serif, ask for their best price. Often, there is room for negotiation.

◆ Stick to your list. Knowing what you need will enable you to approach the vendor with clarity, giving an exact breakdown of your requirements.

◆ Look for free utilities and software. Free utilities can easily be found after a quick search on the internet. Depending on your niche requirements, you can pick up free tried and tested tools to carry out a variety of tasks. For example, you can obtain free virus software or free HTML editors.

Keeping a close check on your technology spend can save you a considerable amount of money in the long term. Be wary, however, of the vendor's sales speak. It's their job to try to sell you the latest all-singing, all-dancing gadgets and they'll do their best to spend your money!

WHAT IS WEB HOSTING?

A web host is a company that basically leases you disk space for your website to sit on the internet. These days, web hosting companies tend to be a whole lot more besides, offering a range of web building and website enhancing tools and resources along with a variety of hosting packages with multiple features. Visit a hosting site and be prepared for some lengthy research as you work out exactly what your website needs and whether what you're gaining is competitively priced.

With such a variety of services on offer, it helps if you know exactly what you need. If you're working with a web designer, be guided by their knowledge in this area. However, it pays to do some research of your own too so that you gain the best package to suit your requirements.

Choosing a website host

Whilst developing your website, you need to give some serious consideration to how you will bring your venture online.

With a website that has been designed from scratch, using a web design program, you will need to upload the site to a web hosting service so that your website can go live online.

There are thousands of web hosting companies offering what seem like almost identical hosting packages. The most important considerations when making a choice are as follows.

1. **Your hardware requirements and type of server platform.** Is the web host Windows, Unix or Linux based? Is your website set up to use ASP (active server pages), Microsoft SQL database, Cold Fusion, Microsoft Access, etc? What programming language are you using? Is it Perl, CGI, SSI or PHP? Find out the technical specifications and choose a web hosting service that will support your requirements.

2. **Disk space.** This is how much space you will need to feature all your proposed content on your website. If your website has a lot of content (especially if using pictures, sound or video files) then you will need a larger amount of disk space. Make sure your hosting company offers packages to suit your disk space requirements.

3. **Bandwidth.** This is the amount of data that is transferred to and from your website. You want to make sure you have enough bandwidth so that you can display your site to all your prospective visitors. The amount you need depends upon your anticipated website traffic. If you expect a high number of visitors, you may well consume your bandwidth allowance in no time at all. Find a web hosting company that can accommodate your expected bandwidth requirements. Check what penalties you will incur for exceeding bandwidth and whether you can migrate to a higher package if needed. Some host companies offer unlimited bandwidth, but do check the terms and conditions as there may be restrictions on the type of data you can transfer.

4. **Hosting features and extras.** If your website has specific requirements (perhaps you need to support video clips or downloads), make sure your hosting service can provide the features required. Also check there is compatibility with the web design tools that you use such as Frontpage or Dreamweaver. Additional features offered may include unlimited email, support of databases, web traffic analytics, content management systems, FTP accounts. Check exactly what you need before you make a commitment.

5. **Reliability.** You need to do some research to find an established and notably reliable hosting service. There are plenty around who invest heavily to make sure their servers are of high performance and that their data centres have a solid infrastructure with back-up power generators and security protection in place. Obviously, such services are usually more costly, but this is a much better investment to ensure that your website is always online.

6. **Technical support.** Excellent technical support and customer care should be second to none in any business, but some companies are better than others when it comes to taking care of their customers. Choose a web hosting company with highly qualified technical staff that offers 24/7 support. The service should have a support team in place that can deal with technical queries within 24 hours and is able to respond to any problems concerning downtime within the same period. There should be multiple ways of contacting the support team. After all, if your internet goes down or you have a problem with your computer, it's reassuring to know that technical support is at the end of a phone line! Choose a hosting company that offers various contact points: phone, email, chat, discussion board or knowledge database that will help you find the information that you need.

7. **Growth.** As your website grows and expands, will your hosting service be able to provide the continued support and additional bandwidth, disk space and databases to cope with your evolution?

Reliable hosting is absolutely essential for the success of your internet business. Make a shortlist of hosting companies and do some research on each one. Ascertain whether they offer the features that you need at the right price. Try to gain hosting recommendations from established website owners.

What else to look for

Here are some additional points you should consider when choosing a web hosting service.

◆ Shop around! Comparison shopping will help you find a good service at the right price.

◆ Look for recommendations. Ask other established website owners which host services they use. Have they had any problems? How were they resolved?

◆ Take time to compare services and costs. Don't go on price alone. A low cost hosting service might not necessarily be the most reliable or suitable for your requirements.

◆ Look for special offers or freebies with web hosting services . . . however, consider if these are actually hidden in a higher monthly fee or set-up costs. Watch out for hidden extras!

◆ Choose a service that allows you to grow.

◆ Use only what you require, but make sure you can upgrade services if your business takes off.

◆ Do a search on the web hosting company to see if you can find any complaints, such as extensive downtime, before you make a commitment.

Using a free site-builder hosting package

If your website is a simple web site with a small collection of pages to promote a service, then you can find an easy website builder and hosting package either free or at a fraction of the cost. (Visit 20megsfree.com as an example of a free site builder and hosting package.) You build your website online, save changes and the site is instantly live at the touch of a button. Easy!

My own writer's website carolannestrange.co.uk is self-built online and hosted by the same company. It was easy to create, taking only a couple of hours and can be updated simply at any time when I'm online. What's more, if I fancy a new look, I can change the template, colour and style of the website. Bear in mind that it doesn't offer all the features that an individually designed site does and there are limitations, but it is certainly fine for what it is. For larger commercial websites or websites selling products or services online, you will need a more substantial hosting company to suit the goals and requirements of the website.

SHOPPING CARTS

If you're selling products online, a store front with shopping cart technology is likely to be needed. There is a wide range of shopping cart solutions on the net and these are improving all the time, with more extensive features and options that will make your customers' shopping experience quick, easy and safe. What you need depends upon the range of products you are selling. You may prefer to use ready-made store fronts such as what you would find on eBay. Some web design companies offer shop templates – effectively ready-made stores with shopping cart and payment processing built in. If it's originality you're looking for to develop your own brand, you need a website that is designed for you with shopping cart and payment processor built in. If you're planning to create your website yourself, the latest shopping carts tend to be much easier to implement. Check the resource section for leads, but try to find a shopping cart that is recommended by others.

The benefits of having a PayPal.com shopping basket

One of the best and most widely used shopping carts which you can set up free is the PayPal.com shopping basket. Even with a little knowledge, the shopping cart is quite easy to integrate into your website. Once the cart is installed, your customers shop on your site and pay you via PayPal.com either with their PayPal.com account or by entering a credit card number. Customers don't even need to have a PayPal.com account to make a payment.

This shopping cart is versatile in that customers can purchase single or multiple items with a single payment. As with other commercial shopping cart software, the customer can browse the site and return to their shopping basket to make amendments before they purchase safely via PayPal.com.

There are plenty of benefits.

◆ The PayPal.com shopping basket is easy to integrate into your website and doesn't require programming knowledge.

◆ You don't need to organise a separate credit card processor. Use PayPal.com to process payments.

◆ There are no set-up costs. Paypal.com simply earns a small transaction fee from each sale.

◆ You have access to all transaction information and records via the PayPal.com site. You can administer refunds and transfer funds to your bank account with ease.

◆ Your customers gain an automated email receipt for their purchases.

◆ There are additional features that you can implement depending on your requirements.

The shopping cart isn't ideal for every web venture. If you stock a large amount of products and need greater versatility to enhance browser experience, you may want to purchase a shopping cart program loaded with additional features. If you're starting out and need a free shopping cart that is easy to administer, PayPal.com is ideal. It has been used successfully on several of my websites.

TAKING PAYMENTS ONLINE

Being able to pay for goods and services safely online has revolutionised the internet and, as a result, the commercial sector has grown considerably in recent years. In fact, year on year, more people are shopping online for everything imaginable from their weekly groceries to that special gift for a loved one.

In the '90s there was much concern about making payments online and the technology community isn't any less concerned now. The leaders in online finance are constantly working with technology gurus to make sure that online payments are safe and secure to avoid credit card fraud and financial theft. Judging by the numbers shopping online, it would seem that more people now have greater faith in the system, but there is still considerable caution. You will need to work hard to reassure your customers that you are using secure payment gateways and also keep your customers alert to any security threats.

Merchant accounts and payment processors

There is a range of online payment processors that will enable you to provide a secure payment environment for your customers.

In some cases you may choose to have an online merchant account. This is a licence provided by a bank or finance house allowing you to take credit card payments, as well as debit cards and e-cheque payments, online from your customers. It is a similar service provided to offline businesses. There are set-up fees and transaction fees involved. If you are bringing an offline business onto the internet, you may already have a merchant account that can offer online payment services.

A merchant account will need a payment gateway, which provides the link between the shopping cart and the bank that processes payment. The customer will complete an online form involving the processing of their payment directly from their shopping cart. Once you have a merchant account, you can prepare your payment gateway to automate your online trading.

By far the best, in my own experience, are the online payment processors. Three of the leading and perhaps most popular processors are Paypal.com, Worldpay.com and Authorize.net. These tend to be easy to integrate into your website and are generally more cost effective to operate.

Paypal.com

We have always used Paypal.com to process payments on our commercial website ventures. It allows you to take or make payments anywhere in the world and the transaction fees are low with no ongoing running costs (unlike some merchant accounts). I have collaborated with several web designers as well as people with no previous technical experience who have integrated Paypal.com as the payment processor into different websites. On the whole, the experience has been positive each time and it's very easy to keep account of transactions.

Of course, it's worth comparing all the options and choosing a payment processor that will work best for your venture.

ENSURING CUSTOMER SECURITY

There is a host of threats that can compromise either yours or your customers' security so making sure that your website and computer are safe is vital.

Keeping your customers secure

◆ Provide a reliable and secure website by using an established web hosting service.

◆ Ensure that you implement a safe and secure online payment system.

◆ Do not compromise your customers' privacy.

◆ Do not spam or send unsolicited emails to your customers. Create an opt-in newsletter list for members/customers.

◆ Advise your customers that you do not send emails asking for financial details and that they should never respond to any emails (however genuine looking) that do.

◆ Have a procedure in place to deal with any security breaches.

KEEPING YOUR COMPUTER SAFE

Computer viruses

The threat of computer viruses remains prevalent, despite technological advances. Commercial web ventures especially are often targets for attack. The fact is that no matter where you are in the world, if you have internet access, use email or share computers or disks, your system is at risk of becoming infected by a computer virus and open to attack through the impact of malicious code. This can result in considerable downtime as you attempt to clear the intruder from your system.

Businesses have been known to lose days of custom, not to mention incurring data loss, data theft or being left with computers that no longer function properly. For the small web venture owner, this can be devastating. Although there are no absolute guarantees of protecting your computer and data from security breaches, there are measures you can take to reduce the risks.

Typical symptoms of virus infection

Because viruses are clever, it's not always apparent – even to the most experienced computer user – when there is an infection. Viruses can hide within your computer system for months. Symptoms can arise though so you should be wary if your computer starts displaying any of the following.

◆ Irregularities – the display of unexpected messages or images; programs that suddenly start or end; unusual sounds or music playing, etc.

◆ System instability – your computer freezes frequently or encounters errors; programs shut down or behave irregularly; your operating system will not load.

◆ Programs are slow to load or run.

◆ Disappearance of data or program files.

◆ Changes in data or content files.

◆ Your web browser freezes or windows don't close.

Watch out for email viruses in the following ways.

◆ Emails with attachments that have arrived from unidentifiable sources.

◆ Emails with attachments from known contacts that have unusual message content.

◆ Contacts in your address folder mention they have received messages from you that you haven't actually sent.

◆ Irregularities within your email program.

What are computer viruses?

Basically, computer viruses are pieces of malicious code created by rogue programmers whose mission is to cause criminal damage, theft or to highlight weaknesses in computer defences. Since the 1980s these viruses have spread prolifically, originally through the now redundant floppy disks. With the advent of the internet, virus creators developed more sophisticated malicious code hidden in the form of downloadable programs such as games, music, software or through document attachments in email.

Like a biological virus, the computer version often replicates and can pass from one computer to another directly or indirectly infecting systems, programs, files and documents. Once such infected programs are executed, the virus loads into the computer and basically looks round to see what harm it can inflict. In their basic form, they will do little damage. In fact, many people find they have viruses on their computer which only come to light when they run anti-virus software. However, not all viruses are so tame. In their most destructive form viruses can cause data loss resulting in extensive downtime, which can adversely affect business. They can also make computer systems unstable and, at worst, can totally corrupt the hard drive and any networked computers. A few years ago the I Love You virus was reported to have infected 45 million computers. It caused billions of pounds worth of damage worldwide. So viruses are a real threat; so much so that perpetrators of computer crimes face harsh punishment if caught.

At the last count, there were an estimated 1 million malicious codes in existence. New malicious codes are being created on a regular basis at the rate of one every few seconds. The most common form of computer infection includes email viruses worms and Trojans. Depending upon their complexity, they will attack your computer system causing varying degrees of damage to programs and the overall running of your computer.

Viruses can be spread through:

◆ email

◆ instant messenger programs

◆ infected files on disks or CDs

◆ exploiting security flaws in operating systems or web browsers.

BE AWARE OF OTHER SECURITY THREATS

The following issues can compromise your security:

Trojan horses

Trojan horses are covert programs which can infect your computer either by clicking a link on a viral website or in an email. They are not a virus exactly as they do not replicate and spread. However, Trojans can damage files, place a virus on your computer or allow a hacker to gain access to your machine. RATs (remote access trojans) are common and often embedded in unsolicited email (spam).

Worms

Worm viruses are programs that replicate and spread usually by exploiting security flaws in computers connected to the internet or by infected email.

Phishing

Phishing is theft of your personal financial details such as bank or credit card information. A phishing attack usually results from inadvertently providing your bank or financial details after clicking on a link in a spurious email. These emails can mask as banks, ISPs or online stores, and the emails and websites can appear genuine. The financial services sector tends to be heavily targeted by phishing attacks. The advice is: do not click on a link in an email asking you to update payment or financial information.

Macro viruses

Macro viruses are malicious macro programs which have an adverse effect on macros, which are simple programs that automate repetitive tasks in documents such as Microsoft Word or Excel. They can damage files on your computer and corrupt data.

Zombies

Zombies are programs often infecting a computer as a result of an opened malicious email attachment. The zombie remains dormant on a computer until activated, usually by remote means.

Internet network attacks

Your computer is at risk of attack while being connected to the internet through networks and particularly wireless networks using broadband routers that haven't been secured. Computers with operating system vulnerabilities are most at risk, but any computer can be exploited. Advice: check your settings. Make sure you have anti-virus software and a firewall to protect against remote access.

Viral websites

Some websites can contain viruses or Trojans in their clickable links or downloads. Often, users are enticed to these viral websites through unsolicited emails containing special offers or interesting content.

Spyware

Spyware, adware and advertising Trojans are used commercially and usually without your knowledge, often to record your internet usage. If you have ever received targeted advert email or targeted pop-up adverts, then you can be sure that spyware or similar programs are in operation tracking your moves. They often appear in free downloads or in CDs given away. Often, spyware is considered harmless, but if it contains bugs or malicious code it can use up your system resources and make your computer unstable.

The main concern most people have with spyware and associated programs is the impact it has on your privacy. Detailed profiles can be built on you purely from your internet footprint and this data can be passed on without your knowledge to a variety of organisations.

DoS attacks

A DoS (denial of service) attack is malicious activity which can be aimed at a network causing temporary loss of service. Such an attack means that your website may become inaccessible for a period of time. If the hacker attacks across the network, it can bring services such as email to a halt as well as temporary loss of network connectivity and related services. A DoS attack is usually intentional although, occasionally, it can happen accidentally. Although not necessarily a direct security threat on your computer, it can result in loss of revenue during your website's downtime.

System administrators can install fixes to reduce the impact, but new DoS attacks often follow rendering the initial fixes useless. If you suspect a DoS attack, check with your hosting service or internet service provider for more information.

PREVENTING SECURITY THREATS

So what can you do to protect your computer and your business from computer infection or attack?

In most cases, taking preventative measures can significantly reduce the incidence of virus attack and security breaches and will save you from the frustration, upset and financial costs that such threats cause. Consider the following.

Be informed

People often fear what they don't know, yet the best line of defence is learning about viruses and their potential impact. Keep updated about virus information and current threats. Place a search on the web for computer virus information and you will gain a number of sites dedicated to informing computer users. Make sure your staff and any other computer users in your business know about the threat of viral infection and what to do if they discover a virus on the system.

Use anti-virus software

Use anti-virus software to protect your computer system. There is a variety of reliable programs you can download either from your ISP (internet service provider) or through established anti-virus packages from mainstream suppliers. There are even a few free services (check the Resources section). Once you have installed the program, make sure it is running constantly in the background. This is especially important if you are broadband enabled and permanently connected to the net. Bear in mind that some anti-virus programs can actually cause conflict with operating systems and may make your computer run more slowly than usual.

Update anti-virus data

Set your anti-virus software to automatically check for new virus updates so that you can download the regular virus updates to your system for the fullest protection.

Back up your data!

Back up all essential files on a regular basis in case of data loss through virus attack or as a result of file corruption from mechanical failure. Copy your hard disk if possible and create an emergency boot disk in case you need to restart your computer.

Watch your email

The major spread of computer viruses is through infected email. All email attachments can carry a virus, even if they have come from a reliable source. Some of these can be inadvertently sent to you from contacts in your address folder who have suffered a virus attack. Be aware!

Do the following:

◆ Set your anti-virus software to routinely check incoming email.

◆ Delete any suspect email.

◆ Do not open any suspect attachments.

◆ Some viruses can hide in the body of emails so close preview panes in email.

◆ Most email viruses have a curious subject line to snare the recipient. Be cautious with all email received.

Choose a reliable operating system

Some operating systems are more vulnerable to virus attack than others. Do some research and consider running a more reliable operating system. Make sure you close any security weaknesses in operating systems by obtaining the latest patches for your web browser.

Please note. Most viruses and security issues tend to affect Microsoft Windows operated computers. MAC users do currently have less to worry about where viruses are concerned, although as more sophisticated viruses are developed it pays to keep up to date with internet security news.

Check your network

If you have a network of computers, make sure you have anti-virus and firewall protection for each computer in the network. For a larger web venture, it may be worth appointing a network manager to oversee network computer security and minimise security threats.

PREVENTATIVE MEASURES QUICK CHECKLIST

Do the following:

◆ Become more informed and aware of the latest viruses doing the rounds.

◆ Use anti-virus and firewall software to enhance the protection of your computer(s).

◆ Update your anti-virus program on a regular basis and make sure you receive updates.

◆ Take care when sharing computers or files.

◆ Routinely scan all newly obtained disks, files and programs.

◆ Be cautious of every file or program you receive by email or have downloaded from the net. As a rule, if you're not sure, delete!

◆ Avoid opening suspect email attachments with file extensions such as EXE. COM. or VBS as these are executable and can do damage if infected.

◆ Educate any staff about the risks of file sharing or opening suspect email attachments.

◆ Choose a reliable operating system, web browser and email client.

◆ Back up all your data on a regular basis.

◆ Obtain software from trusted sources. Buy commercial software purchased on CDs to eliminate the risk of traditional viruses.

◆ Watch out for tricksters! Do not give your password, security or personal details to anyone by email or over the telephone.

WHAT TO DO IF YOUR COMPUTER IS INFECTED

Don't panic! If you suspect your computer is infected, scan your system to check for viruses using your anti-virus software or a free online computer scan. If a virus is detected, attempt to use the anti-virus software to capture the virus and contain it. You may need to obtain a clean-up tool. Should this be unsuccessful, do contact the anti-virus software manufacturer for advice. Alternatively contact a computer security consultant.

 Check whether your hosting company offers any additional security measures as part of their service. Find out whether they have a facility that allows you to back-up your website data which can be used alongside your own back-up procedures.

Unless the technology loopholes are dealt with, computer viruses and computer criminals are likely to be around for a while. If, however, you are fully prepared and informed, the risks to your own computer and business will be greatly reduced and you should be able to enjoy and maintain trouble-free and virus-free computing!

CHECKLIST

◆ Consider what technology and software you need.

◆ Choose a reliable host for your website.

◆ Implement a safe and secure online payment system.

◆ Consider how you will make your website safe and secure for your customers.

◆ Make sure your computer is protected from security threats and viruses.

CASE STUDIES

Tim runs an online car accessories business

Tim spent considerable time finding a reliable hosting company for his online car accessories business. He believes reliability and security are important and decided to pay extra for an established hosting company with an almost impeccable reputation. He has started with a medium hosting package that gives him extra features including shopping cart technology so that he can sell his products online. If the website does well, he can purchase a better package to accommodate the additional space and bandwidth needed without any disruption to service. The hosting set-up fee was low and the monthly payments are competitive. He is not tied into the service with any contract so is free to move on if the hosting doesn't work out.

Julia has an online novelty greetings card store

Julia set up a website to sell her range of novelty greetings cards, but had initial teething problems with her first choice of web host. The site experienced regular downtime when it would be offline for hours at a time. This continued over several weeks and Julia found this totally unacceptable. The host company was slow to return her emails and did not provide a satisfactory response or resolution to the problem.

Fortunately, Julia hadn't started her marketing and advertising campaign otherwise she would have lost money! She decided to ask other website owners for their hosting recommendations and found a company that had good testimonials. Although slightly more expensive, she felt it would be a good investment in exchange for reliability. Her website has been live for a year now without any major downtime.

5
Understanding Your Online Obligations

When you set up a web business you need to make sure that you protect your venture, your customers and yourself from any disputes or legal action. This chapter focuses on your obligations as a web owner and what you really need to know to keep your venture out of trouble!

CONSIDER LEGAL OBLIGATIONS

Although the internet has been around for a good few years now, laws are still evolving and being made concerning what we can and what we can't do when using the World Wide Web. This is especially so in running a web venture. The reason it has taken so long for some laws to be set and passed is partly because of the immensity of the internet and the fact that it is a global entity. As we know, most countries have their own laws which can be drastically different to other countries'. This makes it all the more complex. So there are still many elements of internet law that are being debated and remain to be finalised. However, an internet company that is established in a particular country must adhere to the rules of their country and to any global ecommerce rules that also apply.

Start by finding out your legal obligations within your own country of your website's origin. Your business enterprise agency can advise and you may be able to gain a free initial consultation with a company specialising in internet law.

This chapter, however, gives you some information about what you should consider and provides you with an introduction to some of the main areas which you need to know about before you launch your website. Bear in mind though that laws change so always check that information is still current.

 Join an online business forum. Apart from being great for networking, you can find resources, information and plenty of topical discussions. It's an ideal way of keeping up to date with the latest internet developments.

The main areas

So what do you need for your web venture? At the very least, all websites should include a disclaimer on their site which sets out liability limitations. A copyright notice is also recommended. Business websites should, however, go further in ensuring that all angles are covered from a legal perspective. Websites that collect customers' personal details need to include a privacy policy on site and ecommerce websites need to feature more detailed terms and conditions. Effectively, the more complex and directly customer orientated your business, the more legal documents you need to have in place to offer you some protection if there are ever any conflicts.

There are specialist law firms online that can help you prepare what you need. Some provide free templates for disclaimers, privacy policies and terms and conditions which you can adapt for your own use. Check the Resources section.

The legal areas that you may need to consider for your website venture could include:

◆ publishing law

◆ copyrights, associated rights and permissions

◆ privacy, data protection and confidentiality law

◆ consumer law

◆ libel/defamation law

- contract law

- internet/ecommerce law

- design law

- trademark law

- employment law

- website usability law

- marketing law.

That's quite a list! Don't worry if you find it all overwhelming. You don't need to become an expert on the subject – that's what we have legal professionals for. Just familiarise yourself with the issues that affect your web venture and seek professional advice to clarify any points that need further exploration.

Let's focus on some of the main areas.

THE DISCLAIMER

A disclaimer is a legal statement that is often included on a website, especially one that offers information. It is a statement that disclaims the website's responsibility in case of any situations arising from the published information.

There are many variations where disclaimers are concerned, depending upon the information and the potential repercussions from the information that you provide.

Example of a basic disclaimer:

The website has done its best to present accurate and up-to-date information but cannot guarantee that the information is correct. The website is provided on the understanding that its publishers are not responsible for any loss or damage arising from the information provided.

If in doubt about what type of disclaimer you need for your website, consult a media lawyer.

A detailed website disclaimer may include the following:

1. Introduction to confirm that your visitors, by using your website, accept the disclaimer in full.
2. Confirmation of intellectual property rights.
3. Licence granted to your visitors to use the website.
4. Limitations of liability.
5. Confirmation of any variation and the entire agreement.
6. Law and jurisdiction – how disputes will be dealt with in your country.
7. Your website's contact details.

ESTABLISH WEBSITE TERMS AND CONDITIONS

The terms and conditions govern your visitors' use of your website. It effectively confirms that by using your website your visitors accept the terms and conditions in full. The T&Cs, as they are affectionately called, usually appear on a link at the bottom of every website page.

The details in your T&Cs can vary immensely depending upon the nature of your website and may amount to several pages. There are plenty of free templates for T&Cs which you can revise to suit: take a look at www.website-law.co.uk or www.clickdocs.co.uk. It's worth having the final document checked by a legal expert though to make sure that it's appropriate.

Basically, your T&Cs will include the following.

1. An introduction.
2. A statement of the website's intellectual property rights.
3. A licence that grants the user the rights to use the website with provisions confirmed.
4. Limitations of liability – effectively a disclaimer.

5. Restricted access (if applicable to membership sites).
6. Rules concerning use of any features such as discussion boards or chat rooms.
7. Variation of the agreement and confirmation of the entire agreement.
8. Law – this is usually governed by the legal obligations in the country that the website is based in.
9. Your site's contact details.

CREATING A PRIVACY POLICY

A privacy policy is placed on a website to inform visitors about how the website deals with their personal information.

With an increase in junk mail and identity fraud, your customers may be particularly keen to maintain their privacy in terms of what you intend to do with any information obtained, whether personal, financial or a record of their shopping habits on your site.

When you run a commercial website – especially one that captures information or data about your visitors – you need to have a privacy policy in place to reassure your visitors that you are safeguarding their personal information. Along with your terms and conditions, this usually appears as a link at the bottom of every website page.

The privacy policy basically outlines what visitor information you collect such as personal details collected upon registering or making a purchase; transactions carried out on your website; how your customers use your website (pages they visit and length of time visited) and even information such as IP address (the address identifying your computer on the network), geographical location and browser type.

The policy will highlight what you do with this information. For example, you may use it to administer and improve your website for the customer and for your own marketing purposes. If you use cookies (a text file sent by a web server to a web browser and stored on the browser's computer to identify and track the browser), this needs to be mentioned in the policy. Cookies are used to administer the browser's use of the website and so that the browser can be recognised when they revisit your site. Your customers can choose to reject the cookies by changing the setting in their browser panel. However, this can have a negative impact upon the usability of the website.

What else to include in the policy

You will need to explain how personal data will be used by your website. Usually, it is used to improve the visitor's experience. However, it may also be used to send targeted communications from your website or carefully selected third parties which may be of interest to the visitor. The information may also be provided with statistical information about the users but will also confirm that, unless consent is given, personal information will not be passed on to any third parties for direct marketing.

Other points in the policy usually include a section on disclosures and how information will only be passed on if it is a legal requirement or to pass on to the purchaser if you were to sell the web venture.

A detailed policy will also cover information and clarification about international data transfers, security of personal data (taking all reasonable precautions to prevent the loss, misuse or alteration of your visitors' personal information), policy amendments, visitors' rights and contact information.

UNDERSTANDING INTELLECTUAL PROPERTY RIGHTS

Intellectual property basically covers copyright, trademarks and design rights. By the very nature of running a web-based business, you need to familiarise yourself with the laws pertaining to intellectual property (your creations), not only to protect your own intellectual property but also to make sure that you don't inadvertently break any laws by using other people's creations. Let's take a look at these rights in more detail.

COPYRIGHT

Infringement of copyright has become increasingly common with the growth of the internet. Often as a result of ignorance, some people don't realise that it is illegal to copy or reproduce written or artistic material without permission. The nature of the web makes it so easy to copy and paste material without permission that the incidences of copyright infringement have escalated and there have been more legal cases as a result.

What is copyright and how does it work?

Copyright protection exists as soon as a piece of work is created. Copyright laws work to ensure that creators are rightfully acknowledged as the originator of the work – the work being anything such as a book, article, poem, web copy, photograph, illustration, art, film or broadcast recording. It is also in place to protect the originator from exploitation and to ensure that financial reward is made for further usage of the work.

You do not have to register or pay to protect your copyright although in some countries, such as the United States, you can register your work with an agency to give you additional protection and assistance in case there is a case of copyright infringement.

Copyright is a complex subject and laws may vary considerably from one country to another.

What does copyright mean for the website proprietor?

Here are the main points you should know.

◆ Any material that you personally create for the purpose of your website gives you full rights to the ownership of that material. That means you can authorise or prohibit the use of your original work elsewhere.

◆ You will need to check who owns the rights for any work (web copy, images, etc) you commission for use on your website. The copyright usually remains with the originator of the material and you may have restricted use of it. For example, you may only be able to use the material on your website and not in any print publications. Unless you have paid handsomely to purchase 'all rights' from the originator for you to have exclusive use of the material, keep in mind that the copyright is likely to remain with the originator.

◆ Do not copy any material from any source for reproduction on your website (or elsewhere) without the prior permission of the originator or copyright holder of the material. If you see a great photo or piece of writing that you would like to use on your website, you will need to seek out the copyright owner and ask for permission to use. You may need to pay a fee. If so, an agreement or contract will need to be in place granting you permission.

Protecting your website

Your website should contain a copyright notice to state who the copyright belongs to (either you or your company or the originator).

For example: © The Year Published and Your Name if you are the originator and own the copyright.

A more detailed copyright notice can also be included on the website in your terms and conditions. For example:

All rights reserved. No part of this website may be reproduced or transmitted in any form or by any means, electronic, mechanical, photocopying, recording, or otherwise without the prior written permission of the website owner/originator.

Check other websites or seek legal advice when drawing up official notices for guidance.

What about works in the public domain?

Some work exists in the 'public domain', meaning that the material belongs to the public. This is the case when copyright has expired or when the creator releases their work into the public domain without any intention of claiming copyright. Works in the public domain can be used without liability. You may find plenty of websites offering articles, artwork or photographs that are in the public domain. These may be free or you may have to pay. There may still be restrictions concerning use so always read the small print on any websites or contracts before you use them.

What about copyright on ideas and titles?

Technically, there is no copyright on a title, idea or basic plot. There may, however, be situations where the use of a title, idea or plot could be legally challenged, although this rarely happens as it tends to be fraught with difficulties.

What is plagiarism?

Plagiarism is generally defined as stealing someone else's material and taking acknowledgment for it, or using the work and not acknowledging the originator.

As a website owner you need to ensure that you do not fall foul of plagiarism as well as checking that your own website material isn't stolen. There are detection software programs available which can check whether work has been reproduced. This software is actually used by many educational establishments to check if students' essays and course work has been copied from another documented source!

As previously mentioned, many cases of plagiarism and copyright infringement arise out of ignorance on the user's part so keep the following in mind.

◆ Do not directly copy word for word from any written material without written permission from the copyright owner.

◆ Close paraphrasing of a piece of writing (where only a few minor words are changed) may be considered plagiarism.

◆ Using quotes, statistics or pieces of work without acknowledging the originator or source may result in legal action.

'Fair usage' of material is generally allowed although to what degree is often contentious. In the first instance, try to gain written permissions from the originator/ copyright owner where possible. If you include a quote on your website, acknowledge the originator and source. If in doubt, seek legal advice.

Some may argue that there are only so many ways you can write or present a piece of information – especially for an instructional or technical article – and that some web copy can be very similar to others. Generally, if you produce a piece of writing and have referred to a variety of sources, this is looked upon as research, but if you copy information from one source, this is considered as plagiarism. Make sure you do your research!

TRADE MARKS

Depending upon your location in the world, your business name, logo or signs connected with your products or services are subject to trade mark laws. Where English law is concerned, registered and unregistered trade marks are protected against exploitation.

Another aspect of trade mark law is that of 'passing off' and concerns unfair competition as a result of another business misleading customers into thinking that they are associated with an already established business that has either a registered or unregistered trade mark. If the first business suffers as a result of another trading off their reputation, then potential legal action can be taken. The law, however, is quite complex and you would need to seek legal advice.

Where your own business is concerned, you can check with a trade mark adviser to see if your chosen name and logo are infringing any existing registered trade marks while also finding out more information about the registration process. If you contemplate establishing a website that will one day be a big name online, it would be advisable to register your trade mark from the start.

DESIGN RIGHTS

Design protection covers the appearance of your product or creation. Like copyright, design rights are free and automatically in place as soon as you create an original design. So, if you develop a new shape or pattern, for example, you own the creation and are protected by design rights. You can obtain more information on intellectual property from the Patent Office (see Resources).

CHECKING PATENTS

If you have created an invention which is innovative and new, you should apply for a patent which should give you protection against it being exploited. Consult the Patent Office for more advice.

PROTECTING YOUR BUSINESS IDEAS

As we have mentioned, there is no copyright protection in ideas so you need to keep your web venture concept to yourself during the early and sensitive stages of development. If you have to discuss your ideas with other people, make sure they sign a NDA – a non-disclosure agreement. Consult a legal professional to help you draw up a suitable NDA document.

GUARDING AGAINST DEFAMATION

Be careful what you include on your website! Publishing any material that potentially damages the reputation of any individual or organisation is an act of defamation and could result in a legal case against you.

Defamation is the general term used for anything that is considered libellous or slanderous. Libel is defamation that can be seen or read, whether that's in print, on a website or in art. Slander is defamation that is spoken or heard.

Libel laws exist to protect individuals or organisations from unwarranted, fabricated or incorrect attacks on their reputation.

If you run a website, be sure to do the following:

♦ Be careful about making statements about other individuals or organisations.

♦ Do not discredit an individual or organisation in a way that affects their reputation.

♦ Avoid exposing an individual to attack, hatred or ridicule.

♦ Check your facts. Is what you claim correct? Can the information be verified and substantiated if challenged?

♦ Watch your quotes – especially if quoting other people! What they have said could be libellous but you could also be in trouble for publishing the quote!

♦ Be careful about publishing opinions or conclusions that could be libellous.

♦ Check your web copy carefully to ensure there is no ambiguity.

♦ Be objective! Try to present a balanced viewpoint.

Here are some examples of what may be considered libellous.

1. An unwarranted, fabricated or incorrect attack on a competitor. Perhaps you have suggested on your website that their products are inferior or their company is detrimental to people's health. This could certainly present a libel case.

2. Perhaps you have written about someone who was once an alcoholic. Referring to him as an alcoholic now suggests that he's still an alcoholic when he may have become teetotal. This could give the man cause to take legal action against you.

E-COMMERCE REGULATIONS

Many new internet laws are coming into force and there have been considerable changes in the past few years to protect the interests of all who venture online. In 2002 the E-commerce Regulations came into effect throughout Europe and basically apply to all online businesses.

The E-commerce Regulations apply to those that:

◆ Sell goods or services to businesses or customers on the internet, or by email or SMS text messages.

◆ Advertise on the internet, or by email or SMS.

◆ Convey or store electronic content for customers, or provide access to a communications network.

The regulations provide guidelines and rules about advertising, marketing and the information that you need to provide to your customers. All online businesses need to ensure that they are complying with the regulations.

Some of the main provisions include the following:

◆ The business needs to comply with the relevant laws and regulations pertaining to their country. There are exceptions and you need to find out what is relevant to your situation. For example, businesses that trade with customers elsewhere in Europe may have to comply with rules or regulations in the customer's location.

◆ Specific information about your business needs to be made available to your customers.

◆ There are requirements concerning contracts. If you have a business or customer contract that is delivered electronically, the individual has to be able to print or store a copy of the contract's terms and conditions.

◆ When placing orders customers must be allowed to change or correct their order before it is placed and the website must acknowledge receipt of an order.

◆ Advertising using the internet, email or mobile phone must be clearly identified as an advert and must identify the business responsible for the advert. Any conditions of promotions, competitions or games, including conditions of participation, must be clearly clarified and accessible. The regulations also cover unsolicited commercial communications.

Information requirements

The following information should be displayed on your website:

◆ your name and contact address

◆ your email address

◆ details of any professional organisation that you belong to

◆ your VAT registration number and company registration number if applicable.

Also, when mentioning prices, you need to make clear to your customer whether there is any tax or delivery costs.

Check current guidelines for information requirements.

KNOWING YOUR EMAIL MARKETING LAWS

If you intend to use email communication in the running of your web venture, you need to be aware of the laws concerning electronic communication and, in particular, unsolicited email (or spam).

In recent times legislation has come into effect to protect customers and businesses from the impact of unsolicited email. Any marketing via email is effectively only permitted if the recipients have chosen (or opted in) to receive the information. Failure to adhere to the regulations could result in a hefty fine of several thousands!

We cover email marketing in more detail later. Initially, familiarise yourself with the rules in depth (see the Resources section) so that you know what you can or can't do with regard to email marketing.

Look for the benefits!

When legislation governing email came in, many felt it would be the end of utilising the obvious gains that email has from a commercial marketing outlook. However, it has actually proved to have positive benefits! Customers who have specifically opted to receive your email will be more responsive to what you have to offer. In theory, with less unsolicited material to contend with, more customers will be open to receiving targeted email communications that they have explicitly requested. It means that your email is more likely to be read rather than being exiled to the junk folder (presuming it gets past the spam filters: but that's another story!). With a more streamlined email communications system and many tools in development to further help commercial websites, providing you follow the rules email marketing can prove beneficial.

ACCESSIBILITY

Over the years the topic of website accessibility where the disabled are concerned has been hotly debated. In the UK, in 2004, the Disability Discrimination Act 1995 was amended, making it illegal for a service provider such as a commercial website to discriminate against a disabled person. So, effectively, operating a website that has usability issues for anyone disabled could be a problem. The current advice is that websites should be designed to avoid liability although the topic remains contentious. For further guidance check out information about usability and accessibility laws and requirements on the internet.

DATA PROTECTION

If you hold personal details of your customers or employees, you will need to comply with the Data Protection Act which governs the use of personal information held by businesses or organisations. The Resources section provides websites where you can obtain more information.

TRADES DESCRIPTION ACT

If you sell products or services you need to make sure that you do not provide any false statements or claims about what you offer. Check your web copy and advertising copy to ensure that you are acting in accordance with the Trades Description Act.

CONSIDER OTHER OBLIGATIONS

The fact that you are starting a business requires you to inform the relevant authorities. There may be other legal requirements too and this can vary depending upon your location and type of business. Ask your local business advice centre for advice. Meanwhile, these are some additional considerations.

◆ You need to let the tax/revenue office know as soon as you commence the venture and you must declare all income.

◆ If you work from home you may need to gain permissions from your local authority although this depends upon the nature of your business.

◆ You may need to purchase insurance such as public or professional liability to protect you from potential legal issues. Do you need insurance to protect your products or to protect you from loss of income? Weigh up what you need to have from a legal standpoint and what would be useful to have for additional protection.

◆ If you set up a limited company you have a whole new set of company laws to look into. Again, be aware of legal obligations to avoid any fines.

◆ If you employ people there are more legal requirements to take into consideration. There are also Working Time Regulations concerning the amount of hours they work within a given time scale. Consult the latest employment laws to check guidelines.

KEEPING ACCURATE RECORDS

All financial transactions concerning your web venture must be documented so that you can declare your accounts to the relevant revenue authority. It's advisable to keep this information on file for at least five years. Many smaller businesses keep their own accounts. Medium to large ventures use a book-keeping system and an accountant to take care of their financial records, profit and loss and financial declaration.

There may be other records that you are required to maintain depending upon the nature of your business. Again, check with your business advisor or legal professional for guidance.

 Keep on top of your accounts. It will help you maintain a close eye on your incomings, outgoings and your profit. This provides you with a good forecast of how your business is progressing.

CHECKLIST

◆ Find out what laws concern you and your website.

◆ Take legal advice for drawing up or checking through contracts or legal notices.

◆ Check for changes in legislation which may affect your business.

◆ Make sure that you abide by ecommerce regulations and check that your website complies.

◆ Include the relevant terms and conditions, disclaimer and privacy policy on your website where required.

CASE STUDIES

Isobel edits an online e-magazine

Isobel needed to be clear about copyright of artistic material to protect her contributors' interests as well as her own. She now understands her legal requirements where copyright permissions are concerned. This places her in a stronger and more knowledgeable position when dealing with clients and publishing her online magazine.

Jonah runs a music website with international interest

Jonah's site promotes new bands and also sells licensed music downloads. He believes that it's important to be aware of your legal obligations when running a commercial website and to find out what laws apply within your country of operation. He invested in consulting a legal firm specialising in online law to draft his terms and conditions and all the small print needed to protect his financial interests in the running of the website.

Barry used to run an information website

Unfortunately, Barry had copied and published other people's material on a large scale without gaining permission or copyright clearance. He received many complaints from authors and legal action was taken against him. He no longer runs the website and is in the middle of legal proceedings.

6
Launching Your Online Business

You've researched, scrutinised and honed your venture idea to perfection. You've created your website, tested it and are ready to go live to the world. The time has come to launch your website. So what happens next? This chapter covers pre-launch checks and risk assessments. It also helps you prepare your marketing strategy to start driving customers to your website. You will learn about the importance of your media kit and you'll find advice to help you move your venture forward.

CONDUCTING QUALITY ASSURANCE

Before your website goes live, conduct a quality assurance test. Use your mission statement as a guide and prepare a list of quality assurance markers to rigorously test your website and ensure that it meets high standards in all areas.

Your website quality assurance list may include the following:

◆ **Content** – check for any critical errors in your content delivery. Make sure that all the right information is present.

◆ **Design** – check for technical issues or bugs. Make sure all features and functions are working.

◆ **Technical performance** – check how your website performs in different browsers and at different screen resolutions.

◆ **Mission performance** – how does your website relate to your mission statement? Will you offer your visitors exactly what your web copy says?

◆ **Feedback** – make sure there is a system in place to gain visitor feedback or for visitors to report any bugs in the design.

PRE-LAUNCH CHECKS

In the days leading up to the estimated launch of your web venture it's advisable to use this time to perform final checks, in line with your quality assurance list, to ensure that you are ready. This will help reduce the number of problems that could arise and will, if nothing else, give you greater peace of mind.

◆ Do final checks on the functionality of your website.

◆ Check your web copy is free of errors.

◆ Make sure your email system is professionally set up to send and receive your business communications.

◆ If you're selling products, check your stock and that you are all set to go with your deliveries.

◆ If you're selling services, make sure everything is prepared to offer the service your customers expect.

◆ Prepare your hosting account and set up any important functions such as traffic tracking and ad revenue campaigns (more on this later).

Upon launching your website, you may not see much activity at first. Don't worry. It takes a little time to start gaining results. In the meantime you can use this period to fix any issues which only become apparent when your website is live. When you launch your website to the world, you will be scrutinised by your competitors as well as your customers so make sure that you set out to impress.

CARRYING OUT A RISK ASSESSMENT

Before you launch it's also advisable to carry out a risk assessment. This is part of your business continuity plan and involves determining what risks your web venture may face. The more established and successful your website becomes, the more important it is to have a risk assessment in place so you can make contingency plans to avoid any serious losses to your business.

Businesses throughout the world have numerous threats to contend with. These may include natural disasters, terrorist attacks, death or accident of key members of staff, loss of employees, changing trends, issues with legislation compliance, legal challenges, and so on. For a web venture you can add the threat of computer security issues, computer meltdown, hosting problems, suppliers going out of business . . . and risks pertaining to your own individual circumstances.

It's scary thinking about the possible threats, but by identifying the risks and prioritising them you can decide upon the action that may need to be taken should a threat become reality. There may be some issues that you just can't plan for. However, it's better to be aware and have a strategy in place that will help you deal with any situations that arise. By undertaking a risk assessment, you can also discover where your vulnerabilities lie and make changes to reduce the impact of such a threat. For example, if you are vulnerable to computer viruses you can ensure that your computer is better protected with the latest anti-virus software.

ORGANISE A LAUNCH PARTY

If you wish to formally celebrate your website's launch, make it an occasion to share with friends, colleagues and – most importantly – potential customers. A launch party, even on a small scale, can give your website an initial boost. Book a venue such as a conference centre or even the local village hall. Send out invitations to your target list – especially to any existing customers if you have been trading offline – and ask them to invite a friend. Ask family or friends to help you organise the event and be there to help out on the day by serving drinks and meeting guests. Make sure that you have plenty of literature with your website address available to display. If your budget can run to it, a small goody bag with promotional freebies always goes down a treat.

If organising a specific launch party isn't feasible, see if there is a suitable business or network event close to the time of your website's launch where you could perhaps hire a stand to promote your website. You will gain from the physical traffic generated by the event's advertising.

CELEBRATE YOUR LAUNCH

The launch of your website after possibly months of project scoping and development is a wonderful feeling and a notable achievement on your entrepreneurial journey. It can be a bit of an anticlimax though. Unless you have arranged a physical launch party, it's likely that you and any partners involved in the website will quietly welcome in the celebration of your site going live sitting in front of your computer. Should that be the case, at least pour yourself a glass of wine to mark the event! Take a moment to reflect on your fantastic achievement.

And immediately after the launch . . .

Although it seems like all the hard work and frustrations of design hell are behind you, don't sit too comfortably. You have plenty of work to do. Savour the celebration now because the chances are that you will be too busy promoting and making a success of your web venture over the weeks and months to come.

Immediately after your launch continue running some tests and diagnostics to ensure that your website is functioning as it should. Even though it may have been glitch-free during the pre-launch tests, keep a close eye on the site during these early hours post-launch. You're also testing the reliability of your host too so visit the site at different times of the day (and night) to check all is well.

At the same time, set your marketing and promotion plans into motion. You may not receive too much traffic in the early days, but you should focus on your marketing daily to lay a firm foundation that will bring you higher volumes of traffic as each week and month goes by. Reflect on your business and development plan at this stage too. Visualise where your web venture will be in six months' time. Use this as a motivator to stay focused on the task of accomplishing your income generation goals.

 Where possible, surround yourself with a strong network of friends or family to help you in busy times – particularly while your venture is launching and growing. Having this support in place will prove invaluable.

MARKETING YOUR WEB VENTURE

You should already know a great deal about your target market from the initial research you did when writing your business plan. Your visitors and potential customers are at the very centre of your online business. You will have created and designed your website with your customers firmly in mind. However, knowing your customers and establishing a website that will interest them doesn't end there. You need to develop a strategy that will enable you to find and capture your target market.

Creating a marketing strategy

To establish a successful website – one that will survive and grow in cyberspace – it's important to have a marketing strategy in place to enable you to promote and advertise your web venture to reach your target audience. The effectiveness of your marketing strategy depends upon how well you align yourself to your website's mission and how in tune you are with your target audience.

So, what makes an effective marketing strategy – one that will increase traffic to your website?

1. Start by analysing your customers' needs. Have a complete understanding of your target audience. What do they want? More importantly, do you have what they want?
2. Who are your customers? How old are they? What do they do? What are their interests? You should have a typical profile of your customers. This is integral to your marketing success.
3. Do you know where your customers are? Are they based in your own country or do you have an international audience? Knowing this will help you plan your promotional campaigns.
4. If possible, focus on a niche. This enables you to hone your marketing efforts to a particular sector so you can concentrate on generating results.
5. Focus on the customer sector that can yield the highest sales profits. Think commercially.
6. Survey your customers and research their requirements on a regular basis. Things change quickly on the net. Your customers change; they grow older and wiser. They become more web savvy. You need to keep pace.

7. Target your marketing using your research results. For example, if your customers are looking for competitive prices, then any marketing activity aimed at them should draw attention to your pricing structure. Similarly, if another group is driven by quality then aim marketing towards highlighting the high quality service that you provide. It's all about meeting your customers' expectations.
8. Focus on the marketing techniques you will use to deliver your advertising message to reach your target audience.

Your marketing strategy will *not* do the following:

1. Make your website an immediate success.
2. Make your customers buy products or services they don't want, can't afford or are of poor quality.
3. Mend a customer's bad experience.
4. Fix a problem website.

Online marketing tactics

One of the advantages of online marketing is that your customers are just a click of a mouse away.

Here are some of the most commonly used online marketing tactics which you are likely to use:

◆ search engine placement

◆ pay-per-click advertising campaigns

◆ website link exchange

◆ electronic newsletters

◆ submitting free marketing articles

◆ posting to discussion forums

◆ press releases to online publications

◆ directory listings

◆ affiliate schemes.

We will cover some of these tactics in more detail in this and subsequent chapters.

Offline marketing tactics

Don't forget that you can do a lot to generate new traffic to your website when you're offline. Add the following to your list of marketing tactics:

◆ press releases to newspapers and magazines

◆ advertising in relevant publications

◆ hosting a talk or workshop

◆ attending a network event

◆ radio and television appearances or advertising

◆ a direct mail campaign.

Again, read on; we will cover some of these in more detail.

Tips to make your marketing strategy a success

So you have pages of facts and figures all about your target market. Now you need to action your marketing strategy, taking into consideration what tactics you will use, when you will instigate them and what resources you will need to deliver an effective marketing campaign.

Consider the following tips:

◆ Be realistic. Make sure you can deliver what your customers need.

◆ Your market research needs to be analysed to evaluate your marketing approach. Consider how you will monitor, assess and manage market research data. Will you use an external agency?

◆ What marketing tactics will you use?

◆ Measure the effectiveness of what you do. Be prepared to change things that aren't working.

◆ Watch out for economic fluctuations that may change your customers' shopping habits. What strategy will you put in place (discounts or offers) to attract them to your website?

◆ Watch your competitors. Compare prices, service levels, products, innovations, discounts, etc on a regular basis. Adjust your marketing plan to remain competitive.

◆ Keep a check on your customers' requirements. What's in or out of fashion? How have your customers' needs changed? Don't make assumptions; ask them! Send out a customer survey or run an online poll.

◆ Use on and offline marketing. Implementing marketing campaigns across the media to market your web venture is the most effective. Multi-channel marketing efforts, using the net, mobile, print, radio and TV media, will draw in a significant response. In some cases your customers need to hear your domain name about five times to capture their attention!

◆ Is your marketing effective? Often, you have to try different marketing methods so a small-scale trial will enable you to test your strategy quickly and without draining your time and resources. Remember, things change quickly on the web so what is effective one month might not be as effective the next. Be prepared to experiment.

Starting a marketing campaign

Marketing your website isn't too dissimilar to marketing an offline business. The formula is simple and it's all about numbers. The more marketing you do, the greater the response.

So that your marketing strategy has the best chance of success, consider the following guidelines.

◆ Set some uninterrupted time aside each week to work on your website's marketing.

- Have a clear plan in place for the marketing areas you will focus on each week.

- Build a list of marketing opportunities at your disposal such as link exchange, article writing, advertising on and offline, giving seminars, taking part in chat or discussion forums, giving stories to the media, etc.

- Build a list of media contacts for press releases.

- Keep your media kit up to date.

- Create a list of marketing resources.

- Keep up the momentum, and look upon the time spent marketing as a long term investment in your business.

- Look for marketing opportunities wherever you go. Make sure you carry some business cards. You'll be surprised at how many marketing opportunities are missed by being unprepared.

Don't stop! Marketing and promotion is an ongoing activity. If you stop, you'll fall into obscurity in no time. Set yourself targets and make sure you achieve them.

Using a marketing agency

There's no one better than you to promote your web venture. You know the business intimately. However, if marketing and promotion fill you with dread, consider employing the services of a marketing or public relations agency. Having extra support on the marketing front means that you can widen your coverage and this could create more effective results. It also frees up your time so that you can concentrate on the day-to-day running of your business. However, it will obviously cost you. If you have the funds available, try a targeted campaign. Find out what packages your chosen agency offers. Test the service first with a small, targeted campaign to see what results you gain.

PREPARING YOUR MEDIA KIT

One of the first things you should do in preparation for promoting your website venture is to produce a media kit. This will give a journalist all the information they need to write or report a story. Media or press kits can be produced in a PDF file for instant download from your website or a print version can also be made available for offline use.

Preparing a media kit (or press pack) will save you time when dealing with media contacts. Once you have created the kit, which features your web venture's history and background information, all you have to do is keep it updated by adding new press releases to the kit as opportunities for stories evolve.

Your media kit should contain the following:

◆ A cover page featuring your brand identity with your website contact details.

◆ General background information about your website – date established, website's objectives and mission statement, an introduction to staff, statistical info, facts and figures, how the venture has grown up to the current date.

◆ Details of products/services offered.

◆ Previous press releases featuring stories relating to your website.

◆ A current press release detailing the current story you wish to promote. Include one or two interesting and relevant quotes where possible.

◆ A list of testimonials or customer endorsements.

◆ Any promotional photographs of yourself, staff or your products where relevant.

Web venture ideas

◆ Good with words? Do you enjoy research? Can you create and design a PDF/e-book style document? If you're looking for a small, low cost start-up that can be run online, consider setting up a specialist service creating impressive electronic documents for businesses and organisations. You can research and gather a company's history and extract any interesting stories which would be ideal for press releases. Edit the information to create downloadable company history e-books, media kits and advertising kits for your clients. Gain repeat income from these clients by keeping media kits up to date.

PREPARING A MEDIA CAMPAIGN

In addition to advertising on and offline, there may be times when you need to use the media to gain some free publicity for your website.

The key to running a successful media campaign is making sure that you have a story that is newsworthy. A good story gains an audience, whether it is for newspapers, magazines or broadcast stations, so it is imperative that you find an 'angle' for your product or service and communicate it in the right way.

How to gain media attention

◆ If you already have a claim to fame, however minor, try to use it to gain an angle for your press campaign.

◆ Capture the media's attention with appealing newsworthy stories related to your website. Anything offbeat, weird or quirky provides a good angle for a story.

◆ Do you have a personal story that relates to why you started your website? Is your website the result of a life-long dream or does it provide a solution to a common problem?

◆ Has your website reached a milestone or achieved a special award? Has it helped someone or raised funds for a good cause? Be sure to include all the points that make the story come to life.

◆ Be professional at all times. Good communication is important when dealing with the media. Don't be pushy, over-friendly or annoying. Be polite, efficient and approachable.

Create impact with your press release

Every day magazines and newspapers receive hundreds of press releases from individuals, businesses and organisations all hoping to secure some free space in the publication and hence free publicity. Only a limited number of press releases will make it into print so you need to ensure that yours will create impact and capture the editor's attention.

Follow these guidelines to ensure that your press release is one of the chosen ones.

1. Make the press release newsworthy. Focus on an appealing angle that will interest the target readership.
2. A sales pitch with a thin story will be deleted. If it reads too much like an advertising feature, you'll most likely be directed to advertising sales.
3. To make your press release stand out, provide an attention-grabbing headline.
4. Get straight to the point. Avoid waffle and any extraneous information.
5. Provide quotes where appropriate.
6. Offer access to photographs if needed (but don't send them with your press release).
7. Provide full contact details and your website address.
8. Pay attention to detail. Check your press release for mistakes, grammatical errors or ambiguity.
9. Keep your press release to one A4 page if possible. If further information is needed the publication will contact you.
10. Target the appropriate publications.
11. Once you've delivered your press release, follow up with a polite enquiry to see if the publication is interested in publishing your story.
12. Not all press releases will be acted upon, but if you provide a good story and set it out in a way that requires minimum editing, you have a reasonable chance of gaining the media's interest.

INFORM THE MEDIA OF YOUR WEBSITE'S LAUNCH

Ahead of your launch prepare your first press release that will grab the media's attention. The purpose of this press release is to announce the launch of your website. It should give information about what the website is about and who it's aimed at. However, this information alone isn't enough. To reiterate, the media are more interested in the story behind the website – why it was created, by whom and any significant angle that will turn your story from an advert into a genuinely interesting article for the news pages.

To gain the interest of the publication that targets your customers, give an exclusive offer aimed at their readers. Perhaps you can give a month's membership free, or a discount on a first order or a freebie. Offers will gain your customers' attention and may provide you with more space in the publication.

Your pre-launch press release should contain the following:

◆ An interesting, newsworthy story hook.

◆ The date of your website's launch.

◆ Some background information about you and your website.

◆ Any reader offers.

◆ Most importantly – your website address.

We consider more promotional tactics in the next chapter.

 To gain a better idea of your customers, how they use your website and what pages they tend to look at, it's worth using a statistics program to give you all the data you need to maintain your venture's success. Try Google Analytics as it's free.

CHECKLIST

◆ Create a marketing strategy.

◆ Know exactly who your customers are and where you will find them.

◆ Prepare a media kit.

◆ Prepare a media campaign.

◆ Inform the media of your launch.

◆ Make last-minute pre-launch checks.

◆ Celebrate your launch!

CASE STUDIES

Daisy is launching an online friendship and dating agency for the over 40s

Daisy is using her marketing strategy to target her over 40s customers. She is drawing upon her own experience of being over 40 and how she had found it difficult to find new friends and a relationship. By using this personal angle as a focus for her initial media campaign, she hopes that the press will be interested enough in her story to give the website some needed publicity. She is also looking to offer free membership to the first ten readers of her local newspaper who make an enquiry.

Ross is promoting his website for ghost-hunters

With a lifetime interest in the paranormal, Ross has launched a website all about ghost-hunting and other aspects of the unexplained. His aim is to use the site to also promote his ghost tours, talks and his books on the paranormal. He has had a few interesting experiences over the years in his research of haunted buildings which provide an angle for gaining some media interest. He has prepared a marketing strategy and has highlighted where he may be able to gain some free editorial in publications relating to his target audience.

7
Finding Your Customers

If you want your web venture to be successful, you need to stay on top of the task of finding and attracting your customers. This chapter looks more closely at a range of online and offline marketing techniques. Learn all about revolutionary advertising that can enable you to monitor results and place you in control of your advertising spend. Find out about search engine placement and optimisation. Discover free ways of gaining publicity to attract your customers to your website.

MARKETING ONLINE

Online marketing offers a fantastic range of opportunities to promote your web venture. In fact, for many businesses online, the variety of techniques available has contributed to the many fortunes that have been made. Let's now take a look at some of these marketing tools which you can apply.

USING SEARCH ENGINES

How many times do you use a search engine to find what you're looking for on the internet? If you're like me, it's possible that you use a search engine quite frequently whenever you go online. This tool has shaped the internet and made it possible to find websites and information that you wouldn't have found any other way. It's no wonder that the big search engine companies invest so much time and money into their search technology; it really is at the heart of what makes the internet successful.

For your web venture search engines are an invaluable tool. Register with every popular search engine. It may take a while to appear in the search engine files

– expect anything from weeks to months. This is especially the case with more well-known search engines such as Google, Lycos, Yahoo and MSN. Listings are free, however, so it's worth pursuing.

The competition

The main problem with being listed on a search engine is the competition. Most people will only search through the first few pages of results. When they can't find what they're looking for, they try changing their search terms. If, however, you're not in the top ten pages for a specific search term, it's unlikely you'll be found this way. Despite this, do not dismiss the use of search engines. You can't expect to have a high page ranking to begin with. Competition is tough, but your page ranking will improve naturally as you build your content, increase your reciprocal links and become more established on the web.

It's important that your website is optimised for search engine listing. More about this in a moment! Another alternative is 'pay for search listings' which has enabled websites to buy a higher place in the search engine lists. Some may see it as gaining quicker results – especially if you're just starting out. However, if you actively promote your website online you will climb higher in the search placement organically without having to pay.

Search engine marketing

SEM (search engine marketing) uses the power of search engine technology, engaging several techniques, to drive prospective customers to your website.

If knowledgeable, you can undertake SEM yourself. Alternatively, it's worth looking at the costs of employing the services of a search engine marketing company. The better ones are confident that you'll gain a greater return on your investment. However, as always, check the small print before engaging any services.

It's true that with the right approach, you will benefit from:

◆ a healthier ROI (return on investment)

◆ lead generation resulting in new customers

- enhanced sales

- better visibility for your website.

Search engine optimisation

You may have heard the abbreviation SEO (search engine optimisation). It is the process of building and maintaining your website – its keywords in particular – to enhance your search engine listing and placement.

With an optimised website you make it easier for search engines to decide upon the relevant keywords in relation to your site. When people search, using those keywords, your listing in the search engines is improved.

The aim of SEO is not only to have your site correctly listed, but to gain a high placement in the search engines without having to pay for the privilege. An effectively optimised website will show up in the initial pages of the most popular search engines.

Benefits:

- Gain free website listings in the popular search engines.

- Achieve a higher page positioning.

- Drive targeted traffic to your website.

Drawbacks:

- It takes time to gain results.

- You need to be knowledgeable to administer it correctly.

- Keeping your place in the search engines requires regular attention to your SEO as your website evolves.

Apart from working with your keywords to optimise your website, keep on top of your link campaigns and submit your website to relevant directories. It will help propagate your website.

Choosing good keywords

Your keywords effectively sum up your website and what it has to offer to your customers. However, some keywords are more widely used than others and it pays, if possible, to avoid keywords used by your biggest and more successful competitors.

Careful research is required to make sure that your chosen words have high search volume on the main search engines. You can use one or several key words that directly relate to your website.

Watch for subtleties between words. For example, the words 'artists' and 'art' relate, but one may have a substantially greater use as a search term. You'll need to decide whether you would use both keywords, if relevant.

Deciding on the right keywords requires some research, using a keyword research and analyser tool (see resource section).

Conduct the research and ask yourself:

◆ How many people are searching against each keyword that you submit?

◆ How many websites – especially the more popular ones – are competing for those keywords?

Use the relevant keywords with a high search return, but consider whether you can beat the competition.

Placement of your keywords

Your keywords can appear as follows:

◆ In your website's title tag and meta tags. If you're working with a designer make sure your keywords have been included in these locations.

◆ In your domain name. Try to choose a domain name that features one of your main keywords.

◆ In your page plain text content – headings, sub-headings and within the page text of your website copy.

◆ In your image ALT tags.

Ideally your keywords should appear in all these places. Search engines will only pick up the typed text on your website and not hidden text – for example, within images. Focus on optimising your home or entry page; however, keep a check on your keyword density.

Keyword density

How many keywords should you include on your web pages? We touched on this in Chapter 3 but let's reiterate. Too few and the search engines might not pick up on your keywords. Too many and, apart from having repetitive and unappealing copy, search engines might ignore or ban your site and regard this as a spamming attempt to gain a higher ranking. So what should you be aiming for? On average you should look for a keyword density of between 3% and 7%. You can test your keyword density with a keyword density tool.

Search engine technology has, however, improved immensely and is becoming more adept at picking up websites to list and rank according to other factors such as being listed in directories, reciprocal linking, use of pay-per-click campaigns, and regularity and quality of site updates. So keyword density is only a piece in the overall jigsaw of search engine optimisation, although still considered important.

 Stay dispassionate about your key word results. It's easy to be carried away by the figures as you calculate the potential, but not everyone inputting a search term is looking to buy a product or service. Many are simply looking for information. Calculate a low percentage – as little as 1% – of the keyword search term result as being potential customers. Then anything above this will be a nice bonus.

Paid search engine inclusion

Paid inclusion is another option for gaining a quicker search engine placement and involves paying a fee (either a one time inclusion fee or a type of pay-per-click model) to have your website pages reviewed and indexed. There is no guarantee, however, that your website will be ranked higher. It is thought that it can reduce the time for a search engine crawler to discover your website. However, if you spend time on search engine optimisation, the benefits will be more long term and you will be listed organically without having to pay.

Paid inclusion may be advantageous though to some websites, for example the following:

◆ For newly launched websites which need to be indexed quickly.

◆ If you've found a high keyword term search on a particular search engine and you wish to increase your visibility on that particular index.

◆ Information pages that are constantly changing their content (news sites for example) need to be indexed more frequently than relying on an intermittent search engine crawl. Paid inclusion would enable your site's pages to be indexed on a regular basis.

◆ Perhaps some of your web pages aren't being indexed in a routine search engine crawl. If so, paid inclusion will enable you to have pages of your choice indexed.

USING DIRECTORY LISTING

Apart from crawling through the internet, search engines check out the major directories as a source for finding new websites. It makes sense then to include your website in the main directories as this will improve your search engine inclusion and ranking. You also gain a link placed in the directory.

DMOZ is the main directory. It runs the Open Directory Project, founded in the spirit of the Open Source movement. It is the largest human-edited directory of the Web, constructed and maintained by a global community of volunteer editors, working to provide a comprehensive catalogue of websites. It is totally free to submit a website to the directory and to use the information in the directory.

Include your website free in credible directories such as DMOZ or Yahoo. Keep in mind that it can take a few weeks and there are no guarantees that your listing will be successful. It helps that you submit the right information into the right categories to increase your chances of gaining a directory entry.

Like paid inclusion for search engines, there is also a paid inclusion option for directories which promises that your website will be reviewed within days rather than weeks or months. If you have an overflowing marketing budget at your disposal and need quick results, then paid inclusion is worth considering. Otherwise, hang on to your money and focus on your marketing efforts.

Monitor your search engine marketing

Search engine marketing, whether paid or free, isn't just about gaining a high placement in the search engines or generating high volumes of traffic. It's more important to drive the right traffic to your site. So it's essential that you monitor the results and keep a close eye on your conversion rate (conversion rate being the number of visitors that turn into customers) in relation to the volume of traffic generated. This will enable you to see whether you're gaining the expected return. If not, then you need to take a fresh look at your keywords in relation to your website's goals.

SEM undoubtedly requires some commitment but, if done well, can bring about substantial returns.

USING PAY-PER-CLICK ADVERTISING

One of the most effective ways of driving more traffic and potential customers to your website is through PPC – pay-per-click advertising. My colleagues and I have used this system for various ventures with much success to gain targeted traffic without it eating heavily into profits.

Unlike SEO, pay-per-click is more instantaneous in gaining results and making your website visible in the search engines and directories. Where marketing spend is concerned, many online ventures are increasing their budgets in their PPC campaigns.

Pay-per-click advertising draws upon specific keywords, usually from an advert that you have carefully composed, and is then aimed at your target market. When someone clicks upon your advert they arrive at your site. Your pay-per-click and the amount of your spend vary although you can set a daily maximum so that you're always in control of your advertising budget. What's more, you can track results to see how effective your advert and conversion rate are.

The most common pay-per-click advertising is run by Google.com. You have probably visited many websites featuring these ads and they are easily recognisable, usually in a column of small adverts or as a stand-alone advert down the side or across the top of a webpage. However, the pay-per-click service is provided by most of the big search engines including msn.com and yahoo.com.

Pay-per-click is obviously only effective with the right keywords and if you can convert a good percentage (around 4% is very good) of the traffic into your paying customers. This depends upon having a viable website and a viable product/service.

Set up a Google.com AdWords campaign

As one of the most successful companies at the core of the internet, it's not surprising that Google.com offers one of the largest advertising pay-per-click programs in the form of Google.com AdWords. Not only is it popular but, with the right approach, it's also highly effective in driving traffic to your website and can make a significant difference to your sales figures.

The program is based on CPC (cost-per-click) pricing. This means that the advertiser only pays when an ad is clicked on. There is a nominal one-time activation fee. After that, you pay only for the clicks on your keyword-targeted AdWords ads. You have complete control of your advertising campaign. Decide how much you wish to spend on your adverts. Change the amount whenever you want. You can place a cap on your spend so that your advertising budget doesn't spiral out of control. You can alter your advert whenever you want to experiment with different key words. Tracking enables you to determine how successful your advert is and you are able to analyse the data at any time.

It's easy to set up an account. Once you gain approval authorisation you're ready to use AdWords. There are four basic steps.

Step 1 – target your customers. The world is literally at your fingertips. Your advert can feature in some 200 countries and you can choose from dozens of languages if you wish. You can also scale the target right down so that your advert only appears to users in specific regions.

Step 2 – create your key word-rich ad. First, write the text for your advert. You have up to 95 characters to work with so this is much smaller than a text message. Start by creating a headline and then provide two lines of text. You enter the website URL that will appear in the advert. You can choose a destination URL to direct traffic to a particular page. See the website for more details. Select your keywords that relate specifically to your website. Start by using a few main keywords to experiment. You can always add more later.

Step 3 – set the price. It's simple; just follow the website menu. Choose your currency, then set your CPC (cost-per-click) and your daily budget. You can change this at any time, but start with a minimum amount (say just £2 a day) just to test the effectiveness of your advert. You need to gauge how your advert performs.

Step 4 – finish creating your AdWords account. When you're ready to activate your advert, log in to your account and submit your billing information. The website is easy to use and you'll find plenty of advice on site.

Monitor your AdWords campaign

It's advisable to track your ad campaign on a daily basis – at least initially. Close monitoring will enable you to refine your adverts or settings to gain maximum results. You can quickly decide whether this advertising medium will work for your website and you should be able to do this without dipping too much into your advertising budget.

Not everyone is a fan of Google.com AdWords. Some feel that it is oversubscribed and has lost its impact. Some find that the program isn't effective for them or that results are unpredictable. Others have voiced concerns over click-fraud – when ads are being clicked on repeatedly by the same person in a deliberate action to sabotage the campaign. Measures have been brought in to counteract click-fraud although it still remains a weakness.

Other pay-per-click programs are coming on the scene and it's possible that some other advertising program will launch before too long. For now, I can vouch that for some of my web ventures it has proved most efficient in driving targeted traffic which has resulted in an increase of sales. The success can, however, be attributed to my colleagues who have successfully administered the scheme, using the right key words. I can't overemphasise that the approach has to be right!

Your pay-per-click spend

Carefully consider your budget for your pay-per-click campaign. You'll need to work out:

1. How much can you spend to gain a customer (your cost-per-acquisition)?
2. How much profit can you potentially generate (your return-on-investment)?

Take the following example:

If 10,000 visitors come to your website and 500 purchase your product, which costs £20, the maths would add up as follows:

Conversion rate 5%
Total profit £20 x 500 = £10,000
Your profit for each customer £1

Your pay-per-click spend needs to be less than £1 otherwise it starts affecting your profits.

Analysing the pay-per-click stats on a daily basis will reveal if you're on target with your figures.

EXPLORING BANNER ADVERTISING

Some thought that with the introduction and proliferation of the pay-per-click advertising campaigns administered by the likes of MSN, Yahoo and Google.com, banner advertising would suffer. In reality it has probably helped to highlight that individual banner adverts (as opposed to the sameness of the pay-per-click ads) help a business stand out on a website.

A banner advert is similar to a boxed display advert that you would find in a newspaper or magazine. It is individual to your website so advertises your brand along with your message. When a visitor clicks on the banner they will arrive at your website.

There are many different sizes and styles of banner adverts which usually appear on high traffic websites. Cost varies and usually depends upon the prominence and traffic stats of the website displaying banner adverts and how long you intend to advertise for. Having a banner advert on a website such as myspace.com or friendsreunited.com will cost considerably more than a lesser known website. However, a website with a target market and good traffic figures is worth advertising on so make enquiries with such websites.

EXCHANGING WEB LINKS CAN HELP YOUR BUSINESS

One of the most efficient and free ways of driving new customers to your website is through reciprocal links. This is where you advertise your website (usually a line of text and the website URL) on another website that is relevant to or complements your own. In return, you place their website link on your own site. If you link to the right sites it can drive considerable traffic and potential customers to your website.

The key to success here is establishing a link on a website that is well known and has a high volume of traffic. Once more, it is important to target your linking sites and make sure they are appropriate to your own venture. For example, if you sell handmade wedding greetings cards, then it makes sense to link to sites that cater for couples planning to be married or wedding industry sites. Finding the right sites to link to may well take plenty of hours surfing the net, but is certainly worthwhile if it means gaining new customers.

Let's take a closer look at the advantages of link exchange for your website.

Free advertising!

As already stated, exchanging links doesn't cost you anything except the time to find suitable websites and the space you will provide on your own website for reciprocal linking. This can be highly effective if the website carrying your link has a high traffic report of unique visitors. It beats paying for targeted visitors through conventional advertising and can be as effective as pay-per-click campaigns!

Builds your website content

Another advantage of link exchange is that it helps to build your website's content resources. The more reciprocal links you hold on your site, the more resourceful your service becomes to your visitors. This adds extra value to your website.

Gain a rapid response

Once links are added to a website, visitors start clicking. New websites, especially, will find this one of the quickest ways of gaining free traffic.

Links are similar to an endorsement

When another website agrees to feature your link, it's almost like an endorsement of your website. It says to their visitors 'this website is worth looking at!'

Links are popular with search engines

Link popularity can help with your search engine placement. The more links to your site from the internet, the better your profile on many of the top search engines. Remember to include your keywords in the link text for the greatest impact.

Link exchange tips:

◆ Find targeted links. Exchange links with websites relating to your area of business. Obviously, these need to be non-competitive websites. Each website can mutually gain from the link exposure and drive targeted visitors who are looking for more information on the topic/area of interest to each site.

◆ Link build. Link to several websites that are also active in popularising their links and suddenly you have the potential for driving large amounts of traffic.

◆ Check your links regularly. Links become broken so do check that they are working on your website and on the exchange sites.

◆ You and your link exchange site don't have to keep links indefinitely. Review the links and delete if the link exchange is no longer compatible or required.

◆ You may be able to customise your link by providing your website title and a brief description of your site. Make sure you use keywords and captivating copy that will interest potential visitors.

◆ Make sure links are placed in the right category.

◆ Be fair with exchange links. Don't agree to link and then forget. Make sure you reciprocate and provide a link that is in keeping with the one you have provided.

POSTING TO DISCUSSION BOARDS

Another way of actively marketing your website, albeit in a more subtle way, is to post on relevant busy discussion boards. This is often referred to as 'Profiling'. Interacting with your potential customers by providing free tips, advice and suggestions will increase your web presence. This will work for some websites more than others. To see if it will work for you, it's worth posting to a discussion board to gauge the results.

Here are some tips:

◆ To find relevant discussion boards or forums in your industry sector, conduct a search. For example: finance forums/finance discussion boards if you offer a financial service or whatever sector relates to your website.

◆ Study the discussion board and their terms and conditions of posting before you introduce yourself.

◆ Most forums will not allow any blatant advertising or sales pitch. This is regarded as spam. Many forums, however, allow you to include your website address in your message signature, which also counts as an extra link to your site.

◆ Consider your angle. Be personable and friendly. It's important that you become part of the community.

◆ Provide genuine value in your posts, and people will click through to your site, thus gaining you free traffic.

◆ Fully participate in discussions. Start new discussions. Ask questions. Give answers. You need to be of value to others. Once you are established on the discussion board you may be allowed to insert a link to your website. Again, this depends upon the rules of the discussion board and will vary from one site to another.

◆ If you have the knowledge, become an expert in your field. Post to popular topics and you will gain more exposure.

◆ Keep your forum postings polite, helpful and informative. Avoid argumentative postings or any messaging that places you in a negative light. Remember, you are presenting a public face and any negative postings could affect the credibility of your website venture.

Post to discussion boards as part of your weekly marketing strategy. Do assess the time you spend on discussion boards and keep this to a minimum. Some forums are addictive and you could easily end up spending hours writing and replying to posts. Try to step back after a few posts and reflect on just how effective it is in winning you new customers.

WRITE FREE ARTICLES TO PROMOTE YOUR WEBSITE

You can attract customers to your website by writing free articles in your subject area and submitting these to content sites for free distribution to other website developers.

Writing a good article takes time so what's the point of doing it for nothing? Actually, you can look upon it as a trade. You're providing some expertise or knowledge and in return your website will gain exposure to new customers.

How it works

You write an article related to your expertise. The article should be between 500 to 750 words. At the end of the article you will add your author details – a brief paragraph bio and your website link. The article is submitted to a content site (see Resources for examples). Once approved, your article will be listed on the site and made available for other web developers to publish on their websites. The rules usually state that the web developer needs to include the complete, unedited article along with the author's bio and website link on their website as a condition of publishing.

If a website with high traffic posts your article on their site, this can generate substantial traffic to your website. With the right article subject, this can be an extremely successful method of reaching and attracting your target customers. What's more, you'll become something of an expert in your chosen field so the more articles you submit to content websites, the better the response.

Apart from free content sites, there are other ways you can write to attract visitors to your site:

Write a blog

A blog is effectively a web log or online journal. You can write about absolutely anything and if you can tie it in with your website, then you can use it to drive traffic to your site. Search engines love blogs. This is fresh, original content being posted on the internet on a regular basis. You can write a blog on your website or to a dedicated blog site which then links to your website. Writing to an established blog site will probably generate more traffic so try this approach.

Writing for e-newsletters

Apart from writing your own customer newsletter, you could write an article to appear free in high traffic e-newsletters. Editors are always looking for good content. Some even pay. However, if you want to include your bio and web link, or if your article is more advertorial copy, then be happy that it's being published for free. A good article could be featured, thus allowing your author bio to reach thousands of subscribers (on popular newsletters). It could send considerable traffic to your website.

Some article writing tips

◆ Follow the general guidelines for writing web copy.

◆ Provide a captivating headline.

◆ Write to suit your target audience.

◆ Use the article to give the reader a taster – explain they can find more information by visiting your website.

◆ Establish yourself as an expert. Provide quality information. Readers will see through advertising copy thinly disguised as an informative article.

◆ Use full website links so that the reader can click on them to instantly visit your website.

◆ Occasionally, try changing your author bio. Experiment with your approach.

Your free articles (providing that they have a year round appeal and aren't quick to date) can be archived on websites and reused in newsletters. This means you can still have traffic coming in from your articles for months or even years. Having lots of links pointing towards your website is good for search engine placement too.

Plan of action

◆ Write articles for your own website and newsletters first and, if possible, recycle them.

◆ Revise articles or provide a condensed version of a more extensive article to send to other e-publications. Don't forget to include a paragraph bio with your clickable website link.

◆ Submit your articles to ezines and e-newsletters. However, try to send out different articles to competing e-publications. Editors won't appreciate the same article appearing simultaneously in a competitor's e-publication.

◆ Once articles have appeared in various e-publications (and providing that you have retained your copyright), find a range of content websites that are actively requesting free articles. Check their rules and conditions.

◆ Submit your free articles to content websites. They should send you an email if your article has been approved.

USING AFFILIATES TO SELL YOUR PRODUCTS/SERVICES

Your website can only do so much to promote your products or services. Finding new customers is always a challenge so why not use affiliates to maximise your sales.

To make sure this will work for you, check the following:

◆ Do your products/services provide good profit margins – enough to share with your affiliate?

◆ Can the affiliate earn a good income from your products/services?

If the answer is yes on both counts, then you can make an affiliate scheme work.

You need to be able to offer an attractive commission to gain affiliates. Anything from 30% to as much as 50% is considered good. Lower commissions only appeal on products/services that have a higher retail price so that the affiliate can make a good income on each sale.

Setting up an affiliate program

There are effectively two affiliate program options:

1. You can purchase affiliate software. These are quite expensive and technical knowledge is also required in most cases to apply the affiliate program. You will be responsible for running the affiliate program, including managing and sending out commission payments. This option should only be considered if you have the resources and expertise to administer the program.

2. Use a third-party affiliate tracking company. This is by far the easiest and recommended option. The tracking company will run and administer the affiliate program for you. Affiliate sales will be automatically tracked. Your affiliates can check their sales stats and commission payments will be sent on your website's behalf.

Affiliate tracking companies

ClickBank – perhaps one of the most popular and well-known affiliate tracking companies. They offer a host of features and benefits. They can even take credit card payments from your customers, pay you, and pay your affiliates their commission. They currently charge a one-time activation fee and $1 + 7.5% fee per sale. The activation fee is for each product. At this time ClickBank only sell digital products such as e-books.
www.clickbank.com

PayDotCom – another respected affiliate tracking company that will administer your affiliate scheme on your behalf. They can take payments from your customers, pay you instantly into your PayPal account, and pay your affiliates their commission. They charge a one-time activation fee for unlimited products and $1 to $3 fee per sale, depending on the sale price of your product. PayDotCom caters for physical products as well as digital products.
https://paydotcom.com

Attracting affiliates

To attract affiliates, sign up to a website such as Commission Junction which lists commission earning schemes to interested affiliates.

You need to set clear terms and conditions for your affiliate scheme and promote the benefits. Tell the affiliate what they will gain and make the sign-up process straightforward. Provide a range of online marketing tools that will help your affiliate customers sell your products.

GAINING CUSTOMERS USING REFERRAL SCHEMES

One of the most rewarding aspects of running an online business is gaining customers on recommendation through a referral scheme. You can encourage the process by offering incentives to your current customers who introduce their family and friends to your service. This already works well in traditional offline business and there is greater scope to run referral schemes on the net. Incentives may include giving discounts, cash or a free gift for every confirmed new order placed from a referral scheme. Many different types of web ventures use this to good effect.

 Don't forget to display your website address on the signature of every outgoing email. You can easily set this up in your email program. It's an effective way of promoting your website address.

BUYING CUSTOMER DATA

If finding customers is proving more difficult than you anticipated, it is possible to buy customer data from specialist data service providers. You can choose particular market sectors or demographics so that you obtain a targeted list of potential customers who may be interested in your website product or service. Apart from contact details, it's possible to gain additional marketing information which will help you determine the results.

Should you have the budget, buying customer data is certainly an option; however, make sure you buy from a reputable company.

Check the following:

◆ Is the data collection company adhering to industry regulations?

◆ How and when was the customer data collected?

◆ Has consent been given by the customer for their data to be passed on to a third party?

◆ Are the email contacts from a verifiable opt-in list? Can the data collection company provide any guarantees on the information they are selling you?

Buying customer data isn't without its concerns. If the email list you receive isn't an opted-in one, not only will you have wasted time and money, but there could be legal implications too. If you explore this route, take care.

MARKETING OFFLINE

Many web ventures neglect their offline marketing, which is fine if you are constantly inundated with customers. If you're looking for more visitors though, and simply want to maximise your marketing efforts, you need to focus on the real world offline.

If you think that offline marketing isn't going to reach your target audience, think again. Not everyone lives in cyberspace all of the time and even if they did, they are just as likely to find your website by reading an article about you in a print magazine or finding your domain name on a promotional pen or meeting you at a network event.

There are plenty of opportunities to find additional customers using offline marketing – and many of them don't take much effort or finance to implement.

Consider the following ideas.

Targeted advertising

An advert or preferably a free editorial feature in a specialist print magazine aimed solely at your target audience can increase your web traffic considerably, especially if the magazine has a high circulation.

Promotional freebies

Your website domain name is the key to finding you online. So emblazon your domain name on everything. Include the name on promotional gifts such as pens, t-shirts, mouse mats, gadgets and balloons. Give these away to your target customers at events, network opportunities and conferences. Obviously, these items cost you money to produce, but they can provide a lasting reminder of your website and can help drive extra customers to your venture.

Leaflets

A flyer advertising your website can be cost effective to print. These can be given out at events, exhibitions or even delivered door-to-door as part of a mailing campaign.

Word-of-mouth advertising

Word-of-mouth marketing is still one of the most effective forms of advertising and if your website has all the success factors in place, such as attractive content, functionality, good customer service and offers value for money, then it won't take long for word to spread throughout the world.

GAIN FREE PUBLICITY

1. Think laterally. Find an interesting story angle relating to your website. The more bizarre, funny, interesting or entertaining, the better your chances of gaining free publicity. Write a press release and submit to your media contacts list.

2. Write an informative article or series of short articles (around 700 words) relating to your website and area of expertise and include a bio at the end of the article

with your website link. Submit the article to free article websites which grant other websites free use of your article. This will help propagate your website link. Also, write articles for print magazines or newspapers.

3. Write a book relating to your website topic. Make sure you mention your web venture in the cover blurb or in the book itself. You can self-publish and sell as an e-book or find a publisher.

4. Give a talk or stage a workshop. Many clubs, organisations, colleges and associations welcome speakers. Check out your local library, specialist magazine or newspaper for information about community groups or special interest organisations. Is there scope to run a workshop? If, for example, your website sells craft materials, perhaps you could run a workshop to teach the craft, using it as a means to promote your website. When you make arrangements, find out about numbers of people attending. If your website sells products, can you display some of the items at the workshop or talk?

5. If you have a growing list of opt-in email newsletter subscribers, use this targeted list to generate more business. Use your email newsletter to promote services and products.

6. Go on the radio. If you are a subject expert or can offer an interesting story connected with your website, you have a good chance of gaining a slot on your local radio station. Radio presenters encourage guests to talk on their shows and, if successful, you may be asked back as a resident expert. This works especially well if you are a subject specialist and can offer a question and answer service. Think laterally to look for a starting point. Listen to the radio shows to see which would be the most appealing and suitable for your website's target audience. This offers great free publicity over the airways.

7. Be a guest on a television show. This is the ultimate publicity opportunity, especially if you can appear on a popular show.

8. Network with potential customers. There are plenty of ways to gain the interest of your target audience both on and offline. Online, post to discussion forums or

become an expert offering free consultations. Offline, attend business network meetings, conferences and social gatherings. Hold a coffee morning or question and answer session aimed at your customers. Make sure you have plenty of business cards available featuring your website address.

 Maximise your web presence by using all the marketing tactics at your disposal rather than relying solely on just one method. Keep your options open and be ready for change and new approaches.

TURNING BROWSERS INTO BUYERS

When you run an advertising campaign, especially pay-per-click, keep a close eye on your conversion rate. How many browsers are you converting to buyers? If many of your visitors reach your website and then promptly disappear, you need to find out why.

Conversion rates vary from one website to another. If your website does exactly what your advertising campaign says it does, you should be turning those browsers into buyers. If not, then investigate the following.

◆ Are your visitors having problems using any of the website's functions? Check that all your links and pages are working. Make sure that every step to the order process is quick and easy to administer.

◆ Do your visitors feel secure about buying from you? Your site needs to contain content that inspires confidence.

◆ Are you displaying your products and services in a way that will encourage sales? Tweak your web copy and check the overall display.

◆ Are you offering enough to encourage a purchase? If what you sell is popular, you need to work harder at converting your visitors into buyers. Run special offers, discounts or freebies.

Some visitors will arrive at your site out of curiosity; some will arrive by mistake. So allow for this when reviewing your traffic statistics.

CHECKLIST

◆ Establish your online marketing strategy.

◆ Add your site to search engines.

◆ Look at pay-per-click campaigns.

◆ Remember to market your website offline.

◆ Look for free ways of promoting your website.

◆ Focus on your conversion rate.

CASE STUDIES

Gemma launched a website selling collectable teddy bears

Gemma decided to use a combination of techniques to drive customers to her website. Mostly, she has concentrated on using pay-per-click advertising and this is driving targeted customers to her site. She limits her pay-per-click advertising spend to £5 per day and takes care to track the results and conversion rate. Apart from pay-per-click, she is actively exchanging links with similar collectables websites and has posted on a few discussion forums. She writes a free article column for a collectors' website. In return she has her website link on each article and this has been successful in bringing customers to her website. She is currently exploring other marketing methods and is going to set up a store front on eBay.co.uk.

Mike's website sells celebrity memorabilia

Mike has managed to acquire some Hollywood film blockbuster props to sell online and decides to use this as a storyline for some free publicity. His local radio station is interested in interviewing him for an afternoon show and there is a possibility of a news piece on the local television station.

8
Building Customer Loyalty

Your greatest challenge isn't only attracting customers but keeping hold of them! You'll need to constantly work at giving customers what they want and establishing schemes that will maintain customer loyalty. This chapter introduces you to a range of tried and tested techniques and tools that will help to retain your customer base. Learn about the importance of customer service and how giveaways, bonuses and offers will keep your customers coming back to your website for more!

GIVING CUSTOMERS WHAT THEY WANT

Customers the world over tend to be particular about what they want from a service or web store. And who can blame them with so much choice on and off line! If they can't find what they want in either service or product, or if they're not happy with their shopping experience, they will simply move on . . . either on foot if they're on the high street or by the click of the mouse if they're on the internet.

Your task as a website business proprietor is to do all that you can to give the customer what they want so that they will come back . . . again and again. It sounds simple, but once your website is up and running, keeping your customers happy and loyal will be your constant goal and will not be without challenges.

The fact is that you won't be able to please everyone, but you need to aim to try, even if it means going out of your way. When you try to do your best for the customer this courtesy is remembered. It may even win you new customers through recommendations.

LOOK AT YOUR COMPETITORS

To establish a winning website it is imperative to know how your web users behave. You start by experiencing the internet first hand and taking note of a website's strengths and weaknesses.

Visit your competitors' websites and make detailed notes. Was the site easy to navigate? How long does it take for each site to load? Were links, downloads and services fully functional? Did large graphics slow down access to the site? This research will give you a clearer idea of what the average web user is up against when trying to use the internet. Rate each site for usability and then assess the results to consider your angle of approach for developing your own web venture. How can you improve on your competitors? How can you make it easy for your customers to use your website? These are two key questions that you need to address.

So what are the main threats to your business when it comes to customer loyalty?

Your customers are likely to think twice if they have to contend with the following:

◆ Poor customer service.

◆ Poor after-sales service.

◆ A website that is badly designed and difficult to navigate.

◆ A website that has regular technical problems.

◆ Products that are out of stock.

◆ Products that are damaged and need to be returned.

◆ Poor services.

◆ Poor communication.

Treat your customers as you would like to be treated. Consider your own experience of buying products or paying for services. How can you do better?

GAINING CUSTOMER CONFIDENCE AND TRUST

Taking care of your customers is fundamental to your existence in business. Gaining their trust should be your prime concern.

Businesses that float about on the World Wide Web have an ethereal quality. They can be there one minute and gone the next, which is why you will need to take extra steps to reassure your potential customers. Although credit card liability and fraud tend to be the highest fear amongst online shoppers, the greatest problem is that the customer is understandably apprehensive about dealing with a faceless entity.

Most traditional offline businesses have a physical presence in the form of a retail store, office or unit, where the product/service is on display. This makes the actual product tangible and more easily accessible to the passing customer. On the web your product is a virtual commodity. It doesn't exist until it actually reaches the customer. So it's essential that you make sure your website provides reassurance that you do, in fact, exist and that your customers can trade securely and with confidence.

A website is one of millions residing in the black hole of cyberspace. New customers will be naturally wary – especially those who have previously had bad experiences of shopping online. A web-based business can so easily start up, take your money and then disappear without trace. Fake products and false claims exist in any sphere of business, but it is more difficult to recompense the customer who has fallen victim to an online scam.

In order to build trust you need to focus on establishing and maintaining good customer relations to make your website visitors feel welcome and secure. Vulnerabilities need to be removed so that the customer can trade with complete confidence and have faith in the service that you provide.

Although we have covered some of these points in an earlier chapter, they are worth reiterating. Examine the foundations of your service and adhere to the following.

Include your contact details

People do not trust websites that do not give any form of contact details. A web venture provides a certain amount of anonymity and you need to prove to the customer that you are legitimate and exist. On your contacts page include a snail mail address with telephone (if you have the resources to answer calls) and email links.

Make your site secure

If you are providing a facility to trade online through credit card transaction, or if you are asking for sensitive information, you need to have the latest technology in place to ensure your customers' privacy and security so that they can trade and utilise the service in confidence. Emphasise the security measures in place.

Know your obligations

Make sure you know what is legal for your trading structure and back this up by providing information on your site that protects your customers' interests. Reinforce what the website offers. Be aware of global trading laws. The legalities of trading can vary from one country to another. Include terms and conditions, a disclaimer and a privacy policy on the site. Make it clear that you respect your customers' privacy and will not pass on their details to third parties (unless they agree otherwise).

Be informative

Make your site informative. Remember, web copy is all important in getting your message across to build your customers' confidence. Include an about us page – introduce yourself and any staff. Some brief background information and a photograph of you and any staff will inspire confidence and makes the site more personal.

Give step-by-step information

Make it easy for your customers to order products and services from you by providing step-by-step instructions. Clarity is important.

Be consistent and recognisable

Your customers will become familiar with your website brand so be consistent. If you have a site revamp or revise pages, make sure that you retain your recognisable brand identity. Customers may find it hard to trust websites that are continually changing their look.

Keep promises

Whatever you promise, make sure you can deliver. If you say you can deliver a product or service within seven days, make sure you do. There's nothing worse than letting a customer down.

Be efficient in your communications

If your customers email, reply promptly. If you anticipate a delay, set up an auto-responder to let your customers know. Be professional in your communications and reassure your customers of the service that you offer.

Identify your customers' needs

If your customers have any reservations about trading with you, try to find out what they are. For example, if a customer wishes to unsubscribe from a service you offer, send a brief email thanking them for their custom with an opportunity for the customer to give feedback. Not all will reply, but from those who do it may help you refine your services.

Include recommendations

Where appropriate, post letters of recommendation on your website. If you can offer references or contactable details of satisfied customers, this will help reassure your visitors.

More tips for gaining and maintaining your customers' confidence

◆ Clearly advertise and promote your product on your website, using precise text and images that present the product accurately.

◆ Keep your website updated. Having last year's sales notice on your home page and forgetting to change the dates on any static content will make your customers think twice about whether you're still in business.

◆ Make it easy for your customers to gain technical support if needed. There's nothing worse than finding that you have a problem with buying a product or making payment on a website and you can't find the relevant person to contact.

◆ Offer money-back guarantees and implement a refund policy, so as to offer further assurance to your potential customers.

◆ Become a member of a trade organisation or recognised association to provide an extra endorsement. Make sure that this is clearly stated on your website.

◆ Make sure that the technology and hosting you use are reliable.

Provide after-sales customer care

Initiating procedures for after-sales customer care is an important factor. It's vital that you can deal with any customer issues in a timely and satisfactory fashion. Alas, many internet companies (and some of the bigger ones too!) fail in this area and it can lose you custom. To make sure you're one of the better web ventures, consider the following:

◆ Clearly define your after-sales customer care. Make sure it is clear on your website and that you (and your staff) implement it.

◆ Reply promptly to any complaints.

◆ Be helpful and courteous.

◆ Make sure your email replies resolve a situation and do not make matters worse!

◆ If you resolve a situation satisfactorily, you have an increased chance of retaining the customer. If the situation isn't resolved, you will lose the customer and potentially many more as a result of bad publicity!

◆ Offer goodwill gestures by providing a discount on future business.

Establish your company as you mean to go on. Give exactly what you would expect to gain when you buy a product or service. Use this as a benchmark for your own venture.

It may seem that you have to go to a great deal of effort to reassure your customers that you have a bona fide company, but it will be worth the trouble to gain customer confidence and loyalty.

Web venture ideas

◆ If you have worked in sales you can use your expertise to run sales seminars online for people who are new to sales, or who are lacking in confidence or technique to gain results. You could run online or email master-classes, covering all aspects of sales aimed at a variety of industry sectors. Earn revenue from the course bookings.

CREATING HYPE TO ATTRACT VISITORS TO YOUR WEBSITE

If your website isn't gaining your visitors' attention, it's time to start creating some hype to capture the imagination of your potential customers. There's no question about it, creating believable hype will sell your website.

So how do you create this hype?

◆ Emphasise the benefits – highlight what your visitors will gain from your website.

◆ Clearly advertise your USP (unique selling points) such as specialist information, top quality products, amazing discounts, or anything that really sets your website apart from all the rest.

◆ Create an identity that makes your website stand out. Be different!

◆ Shout about any awards, accolades, experience, qualifications or anything that gives your website an edge over your competition.

◆ Feature customer endorsements – draw out the best endorsements from satisfied customers and devote space to them on your website. A good endorsement can win you more custom.

Effective hype emphasises your website's strengths. With so much competition with millions of websites vying for customers, you need to create impact to keep your visitors on your site.

Make a checklist of all the 'hype points' about your website. Draw on the positive points but remember that any type of hype which captures media attention will drive traffic to your website.

USING GIVEAWAYS AND OFFERS

Customers love giveaways and special offers! If you can combine your giveaways and offers in with your sales it will certainly help where income generation is concerned.

Giveaways may include:

◆ free e-books

◆ free e-magazines

◆ free reports

◆ free software

◆ free internet tools or resources

◆ a free gift with a product order.

If you're looking for freebies that you can give away, there are plenty of websites that offer a range of free stuff. However, it's better, where possible, if you can give something that is original and exclusive to your site. A free e-book that you have written, for example, targeted at your customers and promoted as a 'must-have' informative guide, will have greater appeal than an e-book that can be found freely available anywhere on the net. Your exclusive e-book will be perceived as having greater value.

Special offers

Everyone likes a special offer, whether it's a buy one, get one free deal or a sale to clear stock, or a discount on the customer's next order. Run special offers regularly and track sales when you do to see how effective they are in gaining extra custom.

KEEPING IN TOUCH WITH YOUR CUSTOMERS

Email has revolutionised business communication and has become an indispensable medium for promoting business. This is thanks largely to Ray Tomlinson, a computer engineer from Massachusetts who invented email in 1971. His ingenuity has changed the way the global business community operates. Now digital communication is faster and more reliable. More emails are sent each day than telephone calls, so you can be certain that this has become one of the most popular methods of communication.

The potential of email as a marketing tool for your business is unquestionable and, if used effectively, can add an extra dimension to your venture's success. Here are the benefits.

◆ Email is quick and usually reliable.

◆ Currently it doesn't cost anything more to send emails as it's all included in your internet service provider fee, which makes for a cost effective marketing campaign.

◆ You can reach your customers throughout the world all at the same time. It really is an efficient way of keeping in touch.

Email etiquette

In order to make your communication successful, there are certain guidelines to follow. It is important to adhere to the expected etiquette of email communication, so as not to cause offence and also to avoid complaints or even being struck off by your service provider.

◆ One of the primary rules is that you must not spam (send any unsolicited emails). Make sure that your customers have opted in to receive your communications. Failure to do this could result in having your account suspended by your internet service provider.

◆ Keep professional emails relatively formal. Avoid using 'text' language. Good English is still important in creating the right impression.

◆ Check your emails to avoid any ambiguity. Careful checking could save you from embarrassing or costly mistakes!

◆ Do not send emails that are offensive, libellous, defamatory or objectionable. Any complaints could result in your email service being closed and further investigation into your services.

◆ If you are selling a product or service, make sure that these are available to your target audience and that your customers have access to easy ordering facilities.

Use opt-in email

One of the best ways of gaining genuine customers to receive your email communications is by placing an opt-in newsletter service on your website, where your web visitors can choose to subscribe to your free email news bulletins. Opt-in means that your visitors have requested the email newsletter and this helps you to avoid any issues concerning spam.

There are several popular companies on the web administering opt-in email newsletter services (check the Resources section for examples).

Opt-in emailing is an easy way to communicate and you can promote your latest products, services, news and promotions to existing or prospective customers. You can soon build up an extensive customer base.

Emails can be used for the following:

◆ Provide articles or news relating to your product or service.

◆ Send special offers, discounts or loyalty bonuses to customers.

◆ Inform customers of website updates.

◆ Keep in touch with customers.

You should always include guidelines in the email to allow recipients to opt out in case they no longer wish to receive email communication from you. Add a disclaimer at the end of the email and make sure you include all the relevant information and company contact addresses. This small consideration will give your customers confidence in the service you provide and help protect you from legal action.

Avoid sending unsolicited email

In recent times the net has been tackling the problem of junk mail and unsolicited bulk advertising email. Most ISPs and email clients have spam filters in place to combat such email (although they can be unpredictable and not always efficient or wanted). Laws have changed dramatically too. Anyone found to be sending out junk or unsolicited advertising emails can face legal action and their internet account can be suspended by their internet service provider.

Care needs to be taken with any email campaign and you need to be familiar with the laws as they evolve. To avoid problems make sure that you only email an opt-in list – people who have chosen to receive email. You can, of course, email new contacts, but the approach must be personal and not part of a blatant or bulk advertising campaign.

Crafting your emails

The success of your email marketing largely depends upon the finesse of your email content so care must be taken to deliver an email that is crafted to appeal to the recipient.

The guidelines for producing email content are much the same as for creating a web site.

◆ Good English needs to be applied. Read through the email before you click on 'send'. Check grammar, spelling and punctuation.

◆ Language should be neutral to appeal to a world-wide audience.

◆ Keep the email message concise. Your customers don't have time for overly long messages.

◆ Text should be clear and easy to read.

◆ Avoid using capital letters, which equates with shouting in cyber space.

◆ Use attention grabbing headings.

◆ Make sure your content is relevant and interesting.

◆ Don't use the email to hard-sell. You'll have a better response if there is a mixture of engaging content and sales information.

◆ Ensure that nothing you write is ambiguous otherwise it could cause you problems later.

◆ Check that hyperlinks work and direct your customers to the correct web pages.

◆ Avoid any extraneous detail and remember that the recipient may only scan the email for relevant information that is of interest. Give the customer what they want.

◆ Personalise the email with your customer's name. 'Hi Jane' or 'Dear Mr Turner' are much better than a 'Dear Sir' approach.

◆ Don't forget to include your signature and contact details.

◆ Make sure you have an end message that allows your customers to opt out or unsubscribe from the email at any time.

Email frequency

How many times you contact your customers depends upon the type of business you're running. If the communication is too frequent, it can overwhelm the recipient and cause them to unsubscribe to the email. Similarly, if the communication is infrequent, you will only gain an indifferent or sporadic response to your web venture.

Many online ventures publishing newsletters by email provide weekly, biweekly or monthly bulletins. Regularity of publication will give the recipient an idea when to expect to hear from you and, hopefully, they will look forward to receiving your emails.

Email admin tips

◆ Ensure that you administer your opt-in list, regularly filtering through your customer base and attending promptly to those who subscribe and unsubscribe. As email is so immediate, people usually expect a quick and efficient response.

◆ If you use an email publishing/newsletter service, set up the service to automate your email replies.

◆ Keep copies of standard replies so that you can answer typical queries quickly. It will save you time too.

◆ Set up folders in your email client to deal with incoming and outgoing emails. Save any important email communication.

Producing an e-newsletter

Publishing a free email newsletter, particularly if it draws upon a specialist subject or is information-rich, provides an excellent way of maintaining your customers' interest and loyalty. It is also an effective marketing tool to increase sales and generate additional income from advertising and affiliates.

Producing a regular newsletter, even if it's just once a month, doesn't take too much time. All you need is an email delivery service (see Resources section) to deliver and maintain your newsletter list, which also enables your customers to opt in or opt out so that they are always in control in choosing whether they want to receive the newsletter or not. Most email delivery services are free up to a certain number (usually around 1,000) and then you pay a small fee as your list increases.

To decide whether it's worth your while producing an e-newsletter for your customers, consider the benefits.

1. It keeps you in touch with your customers. Some of them may forget to visit your website and the e-newsletter will provide a reminder as well as enable you to communicate any offers or discounts. Your choice of short articles can help increase sales and you can also include adverts and affiliates in your newsletter.

2. It's quick and immediate. As soon as you have drafted your e-newsletter it can be with your customer as soon as you press the 'send' button on your client list. It beats snail mail every time. No matter where your customers are in the world, communication is instant. An e-newsletter gets quick results too. Within usually 24 to 48 hours you will receive a response from your customers either in orders, affiliate sales or enquiries.

3. Costs are negligible. Compared with buying printing, postage stamps and stationery for sending a print newsletter, e-newsletters cost virtually nothing. In fact, for what you save on these costs by producing an electronic newsletter, you can buy content for your newsletter to make it even more attractive and original. The only ongoing cost is if your newsletter client list exceeds the free quota. Even then, the amount is minimal in comparison with the potential income you can gain.

4. It's interactive. Customers can order your products at the click of a link or be directed to an order page on your website.

5. You can build your target audience through your marketing strategy. Make sure you place a prominent 'sign up to our free e-newsletter' link on your website. To give your customers an incentive to do so, tell them about the benefits of the newsletter such as free offers or discounts. Give your customers a reason to opt in.

6. It increases community spirit. Your customers will look forward to receiving your e-newsletter as it is an opportunity to feel part of your web community. This is especially important if you run a club or membership website.

7. It's easy to produce and straightforward to process. If you draft a simple email newsletter, with no fancy graphics, you can produce the e-newsletter quickly and easily. Your customers will be just as happy to receive a plain text e-newsletter. It's the information that counts!

Email delivery

Some email newsletters are delivered in HTML, allowing the recipient to receive a formatted newsletter that contains more detail in terms of presentation and layout. However, there are many email recipients who only receive plain text email, and as spam filters have become more efficient (sometimes over-efficient), you need to ask customers to make sure your email is in their 'safe list' to avoid accidental deletion.

 Don't forget to use the subject line of your email to capture the attention of the recipient. If I receive emails with nothing in the subject line, my first reaction is one of caution. What is this email? If I don't recognise the email address, who is it from? What is the email about? If it's not clear, the email is sent for deletion. Include a few words that give the recipient a clear idea of what the email is. For example: January issue of Your Business Newsletter.

WRITING A SALES LETTER FOR YOUR WEBSITE

If you're selling a product, particularly one that is exclusive or original such as a course or book, a dedicated sales letter which you can use either on your web pages or in an email campaign can help turn your site traffic into orders.

There is a skill to crafting a sales letter. It needs to have a psychological impact on your customers to encourage them to buy and there are different approaches – either subtle or blatant – to make it effective. It may be worthwhile commissioning a copywriter to do the job. If, however, you have a creative flair with words, the following pointers should help you write the perfect sales letter.

Consider the impact of your headline

Capture the attention of your customers with a strong headline. What will your product do for your customers? How will it benefit them? Condense the main benefit in a short, captivating headline to make your customers sit up and take notice.

Craft an attention-grabbing sub-heading

Your sub-heading gives key additional information carrying on from your headline to clarify the benefits. Your sub-heading works by further securing your customers' attention. Use phrases such as 'Discover how to . . .'; 'Benefit from . . .'; 'Find the secrets to . . .' and so on.

Use product endorsements

A brief endorsement (or three) from a satisfied customer underneath your sub-heading can instil customer confidence. These endorsements should concisely explain how the product has benefited the customer.

Highlight benefits

How will your product solve problems? What will your customer gain if they use your product? Highlight and sell the benefits throughout your sales letter. Customers need to be reassured that this product will work for them.

Use bullet points for impact

Bullet points are a good way of concisely listing the product's benefits. They are quick and easy to read. They tend to have greater impact than endless paragraphs of waffle. Plus customers don't have time to read extensive articles.

Be credible

Customers need to trust you. Where possible, provide quotes from experts and more customer testimonials. Emphasise any money-back guarantees. Although a good sales pitch can work, more savvy customers can be wary of hype so make sure that you remain credible and avoid making any false claims.

State the price

State the price and remind your customers about what they are gaining for their money. Sell those benefits! Also use a price comparison such as 'For only the price of a night out' or 'For less than 10p per day' or similar to make your customers realise that they are gaining a bargain.

Offer a discount

A generous discount on the usual price will provide a greater incentive for your customers to buy.

Provide a guarantee

Unconditional money-back guarantees encourage confidence in the product. Most customers trust that if the product doesn't do what you say it will they will get a refund.

Offer a bonus

If your customer buys your product today, offer a free gift or bonus. Make it clear that the bonus or free gift is available for a limited time only. The customer needs to order now to take advantage of the bonus.

Provide easy steps to place an order

Make it easy for customers to order your product. This is crucial. One click of a button/link should send them to an order page. Avoid taking them through several pages as it can be confusing and it's likely you will lose the sale. One click – make payment – and your customer's product is on its way or available to download (if applicable).

Don't forget the PS

Every good sales letter ends with a PS – a post script final reminder of the key benefits or discounts or bonuses highlighting why the customer should make their purchase now.

MAINTAINING CUSTOMER LOYALTY

Consider the following points:

◆ Understand your customers' needs and know what will encourage them to stay loyal.

◆ Provide a first-class customer service that your customers can have faith in.

◆ Offer regular promotions and discounts . . . but find out what your customers would like.

◆ Reward your existing customers on a regular basis with a discount or freebie to thank them for their custom.

◆ Make your customers feel as though they are part of a special web community.

◆ Offer a personalised service that your customers will appreciate.

◆ Listen to what your customers have to say. They are the key to your long-term success.

 The blog phenomena may not have the impact it first had but it is still an effective way of building customer interest and loyalty. You can keep customers up to date with all your current news and search engines love fresh content!

CHECKLIST

◆ Check that your website inspires confidence.

◆ Implement a customer service plan and strong after-sales plan.

- Develop a programme to reward loyalty.

- Devise your email campaign.

- Prepare sales letters.

- Use e-newsletters to keep in touch with your customers.

CASE STUDIES

Gary runs a website selling computer software

It's a competitive market and many of Gary's customers are web-savvy and know where to buy a bargain. To stay ahead of the competition and keep his customers loyal he regularly runs special offers, discounts and loyalty bonus schemes to ensure that they remain happy with both the service and the price.

Alicia runs a website on natural healing

Alicia focuses on writing informative and useful articles to keep her customers interested in her healing website. As a qualified complementary therapist, she answers customers' questions and makes this a feature of her email newsletter. She recommends products that she sells from her website in the newsletter and, when combined with informative copy, this converts to more sales. This personal service approach has helped maintain and grow a loyal customer base. Customers feel that they can trust Alicia's advice and recommendations, and when they have good results they come back time and time again for repeat orders.

9
Staying Ahead

The speed and evolution of the internet means that you need to look ahead to stay ahead to maintain a thriving web venture. This chapter considers the challenges and what you need to do to maintain the success of your website. Learn about keeping your site optimised for your customers and making your site famous. Find out how to identify changes in trends and how you may need to adapt to keep ahead of the competition.

IMPLEMENT A STRATEGY FOR SUCCESS

Launching your online business is relatively easy; making a success of it requires constant attention and strategic planning. Let's look at the importance of tactics in maintaining a profitable internet enterprise.

Start by identifying the challenges and obstacles that your venture is likely to face. On the whole these tend to be similar to the obstacles that present themselves in any offline business. The main challenges and considerations include:

◆ marketing your product/service

◆ competitiveness of your product/service

◆ care of your customers.

You need to have a clear plan of how you will deal with the key challenges that your website will face.

TRACK YOUR WEBSITE'S PERFORMANCE

One way of staying ahead with your web venture is to have a clear understanding of your site's performance. With detailed analysis and performance tracking, you can make the necessary changes to gain greater consistency or substantial improvements in obtaining and retaining visitors and converting them into customers.

There are many free performance tracking services available (Google Analytics being one that many recommend).

You can do the following:

◆ Discover where your visitors are coming from (via search engines or adverts or website links).

◆ Track your visitors' path as they use your website.

◆ Optimise your keywords to enhance traffic.

◆ Track your visitors' behaviour on your website – pages viewed, length of visit, pages most visited.

◆ Rate any pay-per-click campaigns to see how effective they are and check conversion rates.

◆ Review content on your website by tracking your visitors' interest in your pages.

◆ Find out how many of your visitors/customers are returning to your website and how many times they return. You can also discover if they return on a daily, weekly or monthly basis and how long it has been since their last visit.

◆ Develop your key metrics (the data that records the actions of your visitors) over time so that you can reflect upon your customers' use of your website to produce accurate conclusions. This will enable you to review your website with confidence, make changes and track the results to maximise the key metrics.

INCREASE YOUR MARKETING EFFORTS

Your success depends upon your ability to promote and market your website. Unless potential customers know about your venture, your site will remain invisible.

Many website owners make the mistake of neglecting their marketing efforts. They perhaps have a quick burst, signing up to search engines, exchanging a few website links, or experimenting with a few ad campaigns. Then they sit back for a while or become side-tracked with something else. If you want your website to be successful, you need to focus on your marketing constantly and consistently.

◆ Implement marketing online and offline that will generate positive hits for your site.

◆ Be inventive and a little bit daring in your efforts to capture the attention of the masses.

◆ Experiment. Run a variety of advertising campaigns at regular intervals to see what brings in the best results.

◆ Use multiple marketing options: post to search engine listings, try a pay-per-click ad campaign, post to discussion boards, exchange links, write promo articles for free distribution and look at how you can attract new customers from offline advertising.

◆ Use special offers, discounts, competitions, freebies to gain your customers' attention.

◆ Vary your marketing approach to capture a new generation of customers and to win back existing customers who may have gone astray or forgotten about you.

Review your marketing strategy

Nothing ever remains constant on the internet. Times change, your customers' needs may change and your website will evolve. It's understandable that your marketing strategy will need to be reviewed so that you can continue driving traffic to your website.

To review and implement changes in your marketing strategy, align yourself with your website's objectives and evolve with your customers while paying attention to what your competitors are doing. Your business will grow if you keep potential threats in check and take advantage of the opportunities that come your way.

Work out where your marketing efforts generate the best results. This will enable you to use your time constructively. It's only through constant attention to your marketing that you will begin to gain a real sense of direction and an instinct for any change in trends.

Just because you have always stuck to a particular marketing technique doesn't mean that you shouldn't explore new areas. The marketing strategy itself needs to evolve. It's important to experiment and explore new avenues which could lead to you reaching a new customer base. You can only find out what's out there by reviewing your marketing every few months.

 Before targeting new markets, consider how you can gain more from your existing customers. What can you do better to convert your website visitors into paying customers? How can you enhance sales and improve retention figures from existing customers? Finding a solution here is often more cost effective and quicker than finding new customers.

BEING COMPETITIVE

In the vastness of cyber space there could be thousands of competitors all vying for custom. Arguably, there are far more potential customers at your virtual door because you are situated in a global market place. Even to gain a tiny fraction of the market would prove lucrative. This doesn't mean that you can relax and forget about being competitive.

Online customers are a savvy breed when it comes to finding competitively priced products and services. They tend to know where to go for price comparisons and how to gain the best possible deal. If you're not competitive your website visitors will go elsewhere.

◆ Keep a close watch on your competitors. Have they changed their prices, service options or products? Are they running a sale or discount scheme? What are you going to do to beat their campaign? Remember, business on the web changes quickly and you need to be several steps ahead.

◆ If you can't beat the price, offer your customer more. Provide a free e-book or gift or bonus incentive if they shop with you.

◆ Don't compromise your service in order to be more competitive. Customers generally prefer quality and reliability first.

Web venture ideas

◆ If you're looking for products to sell online, consider what will be easy to deliver and what will bring in repeat custom. Products such as hair and body care items, food and health supplements, art and craft materials, cleaning products and the like all have potential to keep your customers coming back to order more when they run out. Look at specialising in a particular item to give your website a niche.

APPLY SUCCESS TACTICS

Whether you are a sole trader or a large enterprise, the strategic planning for success remains the same. Dedicate time each week/month to your success tactics. Are your procedures working? Are you achieving your set goals? If not, then review your strategies and implement the necessary changes to tackle any problems that arise.

Being a successful web entrepreneur requires skill, instinct and action to put in place the plans, as and when needed, to ensure your venture achieves its aims. In an ever-evolving internet, careful planning is essential to your website's long term presence and profitability. So plan strategically. It will make a difference to your future sustainability.

- Commit to a success strategy plan.

- Review your website's visitor statistics on a regular basis.

- Keep up to date with industry news and changes which may affect your web venture.

- Check your immediate competitors often to ensure that you remain competitive.

- Plan ahead for market changes and seasonal fluctuations.

- Ensure that your technology is still up to speed and is suitable for your customers' requirements.

- Distribute customer surveys on an occasional basis to gain valuable feedback about your customers' requirements and whether your website still lives up to their expectations and needs.

- Be innovative in the way you advertise your web venture. Market the site constantly.

- Be prepared for every eventuality. Business changes quickly on the internet and you need to be able to react to changes just as quickly.

REVIEW YOUR WEBSITE

After a few months of running your website you should have a clear picture of how well the venture is doing. A review, at least every six months, will enable you to implement changes or action to make your site more successful.

Check online traffic statistics

Your online traffic statistics will offer fascinating and revealing information about the popularity of each page on your website and where your visitors are coming from. Make sure that your tracking statistics are optimised so that you can obtain relevant data about your traffic to help you plan your website revisions.

Survey your customers

An online or email customer survey will provide you with valuable information and statistics on your site's usability. It will give you an accurate picture of whether your website is doing what your customers want. Make the survey clear. Ask your visitors specific questions on functionality. Findings can then be used to make the necessary changes to improve the website user's experience. Run a survey on a regular basis, perhaps offering a prize draw as an incentive to your visitors.

Making changes to your website

If, from your research, you decide that changes are needed to enhance the success of your venture, make sure that you place your customers' needs first. Often, after checking similar websites, there may be a tendency to want to outdo your competitors in terms of style by including the most amazing graphics and animations, but is this what your customers want? Perhaps you're considering implementing new technology within the website, but will your customers be up to speed so that they can benefit from its use? Keep in mind that change in technology happens so quickly, but the web user isn't as quick to change.

For your business to survive on the internet, investing time and effort to gauge usability issues is a primary goal. It isn't necessarily the panacea to solve all e-commerce problems, but certainly has its place in the grand scheme of doing business online. With fierce global competition, can you really afford to lose any custom? The answer should be a resounding 'no' – so get your priorities right and provide a website that your customers will save to their favourites list.

Give your customers the opportunity to provide feedback and review their comments carefully. You may find that your customers offer some interesting suggestions that you might not have thought about. Give each feedback topic full consideration and make a list of ideas which can be implemented at the next website update.

MAKE YOUR WEBSITE FAMOUS

You've launched your website and have started your marketing strategy with a vengeance. You are signing up to search engines, posting to forums, linking to other websites and using every opportunity to promote your venture and let the world know of its existence. Traffic is starting to trickle in but you're not gaining the impact that you desire. It's time to launch the next phase of your marketing strategy to lift you out of the cyberspace black hole so you can become the brightest star on the internet.

Making your website famous requires some innovative thinking and a pinch of daring to take your promotional campaign to another level. Although you literally have the world at your virtual shop door, your target audience won't recognise you're there until a beacon is set in place and masses start talking about you.

To gain worldwide fame you need to have a website that has mass appeal. You don't want the world at your door if you only intend to offer a localised service. If your site qualifies for mass attention, then you can start hatching a plan that will grab you extensive media exposure.

Identify if your venture has what it takes to be famous. Consider the following questions:

1. Does your web venture offer a unique product?
2. Is your product or service newsworthy?
3. Do you have specialist knowledge about your product/service?
4. Is your website original or innovative?
5. Does your website have national or worldwide appeal?

If you have answered yes to any of these, then you have a starting point. You now have to find an angle or approach that is different to any of your competitors' and prepare yourself for your quest to gain mass media attention.

How websites have attained fame

Take a look at the history behind many of the websites that have become household names. Many sites have grown organically online and a good idea often catches on through word of mouth (or email). However, many have taken advantage of a variety of mass market media opportunities. Some lacking a newsworthy angle invest in advertising campaigns on television or radio, or in national or international publications. Those that have an appealing story angle, however, can capitalise on this and set a publicity campaign in motion.

A good example of someone who used the mass media to gain free and extensive publicity was the young entrepreneur mentioned in Chapter 1. Alex Tew, founder of the million dollar home page, used the story angle of selling web space to pay his way through university. The concept was simple – so simple that without any media interest it may not have been successful.

However, to make the site famous and attract advertisers to succeed in his goal, he needed to generate mass publicity. So he started a media campaign which involved a publicity tour. He managed to appear on a variety of television programmes both in the UK and USA to enlighten the world about what he was trying to achieve. It highlighted the plight of students having to cope with debt, but also launched his career as a new internet entrepreneur. Traffic to his million dollar web page spiked and businesses purchased web space accordingly, knowing it was a good deal for them because of all the publicity. Effectively, Alex Tew's website worked because he made it famous.

Whether you invest in advertising or use an original angle to gain you free publicity, what you do offline is just as important as what you do online. The more creative you are in your approach to attracting the masses to your website, the greater your chance of success.

As any successful entrepreneur will tell you, thinking laterally to generate ideas will help your business proliferate and succeed. Often, the more wacky or unusual ideas are what will gain results, but it's what you do with the ideas that will make the difference. You need to be audacious, confident and a little daring to be the public face of your website so that you can actively publicise your venture and make it stand out from any competition. You need to create impact and turn your website – and even yourself – into a celebrity in the making.

Gaining mass exposure

Find a newsworthy, captivating story with mass market appeal relating to your website and you can gain valuable free publicity for your venture. Look for innovative angles. Are you selling a unique product? Are you offering an original service? Is your website topical? Could you be interviewed or featured in a television show? Can you become an expert and present or appear as an expert on a mainstream television or radio show? Could you write a specialist column for a mainstream publication in return for a website link? Think about your entry point – the idea that will gain you mass market attention.

Consider your strengths to find a free promotional angle

Perhaps you run a venture that sells finance, legal or property services. Could you offer a free advice line on your radio station or column in the newspapers, using your specialist knowledge? This can be exchanged for advertising. Imagine the publicity you could gain in return for just a little bit of time and effort!

Maybe you're an artist, craft-maker or photographer selling your work on the web. If what you do is different, or if you've won an award or are producing something unique then this is more newsworthy and you could put yourself forward to be interviewed for regional television, radio or newspaper. Consider every angle in your quest for fame.

What if you're an inventor and have a revolutionary product? If it's something different, approach the media to line up interviews. Perhaps there is a television show dedicated to new gadgets or businesses that you could appear on. Give talks at universities. The more people who see and successfully use your invention, the more people will talk about it. Talk is definitely cheap in terms of promotion and can spread as quickly as a virus!

Use a public relations agency

If you have the potential to be of mass media interest, it's worth consulting a public relations agency to help you line up interviews or organise a publicity tour. If you don't have media contacts on a national or international scale, this approach could prove to be invaluable and more successful in gaining results than trying to organise all the contacts yourself. Have a clear outline of your story and approach. A PR consultant will work with you to hone your story and establish media contacts to suit. Assess the costs involved from the outset.

Organise a publicity tour

Think about where your target audience is. Are you selling products of interest to school age children? Perhaps you have written a book for children which you are promoting through your website. A good way of increasing sales is organising an author tour via schools. You can read a sample from your book and organise a question and answer session. Print bookmarks with your book's title and your website address as free giveaways for all the children. Perhaps your target audience is college students. Again, see if you can arrange a tour or workshop in all the main colleges. The best promotional tours are visits to radio and television stations throughout the country and overseas to give interviews relating to your website story. Speaking at major business conferences is also effective.

Publicity tours will require a budget, but if planned well it needn't be too expensive and you can include this as a business expense.

More ways of gaining exposure

Consider the following ideas, some of which require investment, to direct customers to your website.

1. Place advertising on your vehicle. While you're out on the road or parked on the high street, your website address and logo either as a window label or more prominent signage on your vehicle can provide valuable exposure.

2. Sponsor a sports event. Your name will be around at every opportunity. You only have to look at a major event such as the Tour de France to see what sponsorship can do. However, start off locally unless you have the funds to consider supporting a more ambitious project.

3. Take part in exhibitions or conferences that give you the opportunity to promote your venture. Use inexpensive marketing gimmicks – free pens, coasters, bookmarks – to spread the name of your web venture.

4. Support a worthy cause. Some may consider this idea contentious, but if your heart is truly behind the good cause and you give generously in return, this can place your web venture in a positive light.

5. Arrange a marketing stunt! Make sure your event is legal, safe and has the required permissions. Try a mobile road show. Tour major cities to promote your product and services while handing out giveaways such as balloons, pens, t-shirts, etc emblazoned with your website's name. Do something memorable to gain attention and to encourage television coverage. Make sure the media are aware of your event or stunt in advance.

Competing for media attention against the giants in business isn't easy, but creative thinking even on a modest budget can take you far in your campaign to gain mass exposure for your web venture.

Develop a mass media plan featuring a list of promotional strategies. You may need to experiment and come up with a few ideas before you settle on the one that will work. Focus your marketing efforts. Be consistent. Gain publicity advice where possible. With determination and lateral thinking, opportunities will come your way to turn your unknown website into a household name.

REVIEW YOUR PRODUCT/SERVICE

Once you have been established a while, review your products or services. Customers' needs change and so do fashions and trends. If you're selling products you may have to introduce new lines. A service-based business may need to be revised to stay fresh and useful.

To help you keep a check, reflect upon the following:

◆ Are your products still what the customer wants?

◆ Do you have products that go out of fashion? If so, do you have other products to replace them?

◆ Are your services in touch with your customers' requirements?

◆ Have you noticed which products/services are underused?

◆ Can you evolve your web venture so that it always stays fresh and contemporary to appeal to its visitors?

Web venture ideas

◆ Could you sell products required by other businesses or industries? Mundane but essential products often sell well. Look at cardboard packaging; printed paper bags; components for a specialised industry; workers' safety wear; office supplies; retailers' supplies; and so on. Draw upon any experience you have in a particular sector.

CHECKLIST

◆ Review marketing strategy.

◆ Check your competition.

◆ Review products or services offered.

◆ Increase promotion efforts to make your website more successful.

◆ Make your website famous!

CASE STUDIES

Edward has an online comic store

For over a year Edward has been running his online comic store. The venture is progressing well and he has a healthy subscriber list. He doesn't want to be complacent about the website though and is conscious of the competition. He has decided to review his marketing strategy and also conduct a customer survey to gain some feedback on the effectiveness of the website. He feels that the feedback will enable him to identify any weak areas and plan a course of action to resolve any issues.

Stephanie runs an online property advice forum

Stephanie launched her online property advice forum a year ago. Although traffic has been consistent, she feels that more needs to be done to make the website well known. She has hatched a plan to do more offline advertising and promotion. She has contacted her local radio station and aims to offer a weekly property advice question and answer session on the radio for the next six weeks. She is also considering writing a book about buying and selling property abroad, which she believes will help promote her web venture.

10
Preparing for Growth

Once your web venture is firmly established you will be in a strong position to consider your venture's growth potential. This chapter looks at your development plan and considers staff recruitment, premises and technology issues. Discover how to grow your web venture without creating problems along the way.

EXPLORING THE POTENTIAL FOR GROWTH

With the world accessible from your keyboard, if your product or service has a global audience the potential for growth is phenomenal. Even if your web business is aimed at one country or region your web presence still has great growth possibilities enabling you to reach your maximum potential.

A couple of questions for you.

Question 1: how much do you want your website to grow?

It's an easy question, but not so easy to answer. You would think that most people want their web venture to be a global success so that they can make amazing amounts of income and achieve fame. Income is very nice, but not everyone wants the huge responsibility of running a million-dollar company. And, as for fame, not everyone wants to be famous. Reflect on this and what you want from your web venture. Perhaps you're happy that it will make you a good full or part-time annual income. Or maybe you do want to gain global recognition and the entrepreneur's lifestyle to go with it. Be clear about your vision for your company's future.

Question 2: do you have a clear plan for your venture's growth?

If you have managed to go as far as establishing a website that is generating customers and income, then you should have a development plan in place to chart your growth from one year to the next. Your development plan needs to reflect upon the changing needs of your business during your growth and what action needs to be implemented so that you achieve your goals. This plan should also include contingencies in case of the unexpected. Markets change. Business evolves. Your own personal situation may change. Actively reflect on all the possibilities because the better prepared you are, the better your chances of being able to adapt and survive when change comes your way.

Now let's look at a possible scenario which may come your way.

ARE YOU PREPARED FOR AN INTERNET BOOM?

There could easily be a boom in internet trade. It is, after all, increasing month by month. However, it's just as likely that you could experience a boom in trade for your own website – especially if it's highly popular and addictive to your target audience. So are you ready for an upturn in internet trade? If you're ready, the more likely you will profit. If not, you could be in trouble.

Three months on the net is equivalent to about a year in real time; that's how quickly things move on the web, so being several steps ahead in your website's planning to anticipate growth is vital to your success.

Answer these questions.

◆ Is your website ready to capitalise on a sudden upturn in trade?

◆ Could your site cope with larger volumes of traffic?

◆ Is your website infrastructure sound?

◆ Do you have the resources to hold more significant stock or provide the customer service level needed?

◆ Could you cope with a sudden influx of enquiries or orders?

It's inspiring to imagine a scenario where customers start flooding to your website. The potential profit could be staggering. However, it could also be your worst nightmare if you're not prepared.

So what can you do to make sure you're ready to take advantage of an upturn in business?

The key to success is being prepared for every eventuality and basically making certain that your venture can adequately cope with the possible increase in trade without it having an adverse effect on the service you provide. It's all down to careful planning from the outset. And if you don't have a development plan in place, now is a good time to draft one.

Let's take a look at some of the key points that you will need to consider to prepare for an internet boom.

1. Technology

Your website is only as good as the company that hosts it. You can have a fantastic site and the product or service to match, but if your website is constantly unavailable or is riddled with technical issues, you will lose custom and credibility. It's prudent that you ensure that your hosting service is reliable and that you can quickly upgrade your hosting package as soon as you need more bandwidth. Talk with your hosting company to gain reassurance about what you can do if web traffic increases beyond your current expectations. Know your options now so you can plan ahead. Also, keep in touch with your web development team and check your web statistics regularly to see if there are any traffic spikes or interesting developments.

2. How will your customers find you?

Cyberspace is vast and to be recognised you need an infallible marketing campaign that also extends offline to capture your audience. Increase your online and offline visibility using the marketing and promotional techniques mentioned. If there is an internet boom you can be sure that your competitors will also be vying for higher visibility through search engine placement and other advertising schemes.

3. Is your customer service adequate?

A sudden influx of queries or orders will place your customer services under pressure – especially if you're a sole trader or only have a small team working with you. Planning ahead will enable you to know when it's time to recruit any additional help or employ staff. It will help you understand when you're at the limits of what you can do within the given time frame. If you don't have the resources to cope with the demands on customer services, you will lose business. Make sure you prepare!

4. Do you have enough stock?

If you sell products you will need to keep a close check on your stock. You can't fulfil orders if you don't have the products. Can you rely on your supplier to provide the extra stock? If you manufacture your own products, can you keep up with the demand? Plan ahead. Discuss growth potential with a business adviser. You may need to consider financing the growth or outsourcing work.

5. Recruiting staff

As your website venture grows you may need to consider employing staff for the first time. Plan ahead so that you know where to recruit your staff. Be familiar with employment law so that you are not overwhelmed with the paperwork. Seek advice from a recruitment specialist or business adviser in advance. You may need to take on additional staff at a moment's notice to deal with extra orders and order fulfilment. By being prepared for this, you'll save time and avoid any disruption to your business.

6. Finance considerations

You may need to finance your growth to take your business to the next level of operation. If you have devised a business development plan and cash flow forecast, and have kept on top of your accounting, you will know exactly what you need to finance extra stock or premises. Meet with your accountant and financiers where appropriate so that they are aware of the possible demands. It will also alert you to any issues or financial limitations.

7. Communicate

Keep everyone informed about how the extra demands will affect the business. Talk to staff, suppliers and customers as open communication will inspire confidence. Be organised in your approach; you'll need to observe developments closely and be ready to act quickly.

Look forward

It's difficult to predict an internet boom, but you can be sure that if you're on top of your marketing efforts, and you're doing everything right, your web venture is likely to grow. It's the rate of growth that can be challenging to prepare for. It helps to have the skill of a visionary although you will start to develop a gut instinct as you become established in cyberspace. By simply analysing your website's performance and staying alert on the latest web trends, you can confidently action your well prepared plans when needed. Looking forward and being ready to react to change will give you an edge over your competitors.

Although you may have big ideas for your web venture, take one step at a time. Don't overstretch yourself. Let the venture grow at a rate that is manageable – particularly from a financial outlook but also in terms of time and resources.

Web venture ideas

◆ Printed products are still very much in demand. Whenever I visit business tender forums, many business owners are looking for quotes for printed leaflets, business cards, brochures and promotional items such as printed pens, balloons, mouse mats, t-shirts and a variety of gadgets. Although competitive, printing services remain in demand. Businesses still need to promote their services offline. Perhaps you can specialise in an area of printing such as creating and printing micro-brochures. How about t-shirts, perhaps incorporating your own designs? Printed baseball caps remain ever popular. Look for a niche.

ATTRACTING ADVERTISERS TO YOUR WEBSITE

An established website, with growing new and repeat traffic, has the potential to generate additional revenue from advertising. With the right approach you can attract advertisers who will pay a monthly or one-off fee to place their advert (display, banner or text advert) on your website. It all sounds relatively easy, but to win the advertiser's allocated budget you need to prove that your website is the place to be seen.

Before you start the task of attracting suitable advertisers to your website, you need to study your web traffic statistics to confirm just how good an advertising proposition you can offer.

Analysing your site's traffic statistics

Your advertisers will want to know the following:

◆ How much traffic does your site generate? Break this down to daily, weekly and monthly figures over the course of a year.

◆ What percentage of this traffic is unique visitors versus repeat visitors?

◆ Which are your most popular pages?

◆ What is the unique visitor count for each page of your site?

Identifying visitor demographics

With the right package of traffic analysing tools you can identify your visitor demographics. Apart from numbers of visitors, your advertisers will also want to know that they will be investing in an advert that reaches their target customers. Website demographics will confirm who your customers are, where they come from and may even give additional background information, including the technical specifications of the computer they use.

Any potential advertiser will find this information relevant and will carefully scrutinise it before making a decision to advertise with you.

Apart from traffic analysers, you can collect additional information about your visitors by running regular online polls or surveys. Of course, if you intend to use any information gathered, you will need to mention this to your customers in your terms.

Advertisers need to be convinced that your visitors are good prospects so demographic information is invaluable, but they will obviously be able to make an informed decision by the relevance of your website (what you do and the content on your site).

The great advantage of the internet is that no other medium can present such definitive data, thus generating income from targeted advertising can be potentially lucrative. Once you have a clear command of your website's statistics, you can work out your advertising packages.

Advertising packages

Based on the statistical information collated from your site's traffic records, you can decide upon the pricing of your adverts and the packages you are able to offer.

A typical advertising package may consist of a prime, standard and basic advert option. Prices of these three options will be determined by the advert size, features and where it will be placed on your site. The prime adverts will feature on your most popular pages in a good position and will be the most expensive.

Where pricing is concerned, be guided by what other similar websites charge.

Depending upon the technology, services or skills you have at your disposal, you can offer more sophisticated advertising options where advertisers pay-per-click.

Some considerations:

◆ Will your customers need to provide the formatted advert or can you or your designer offer an advert design service?

◆ Will the advert be animated? Animation can grab the visitor's attention.

◆ Will the advert remain constant in its position on the website or will it alternate with other adverts?

Prepare an advertising kit

Once you have your site's demographics and traffic statistics and you have decided upon advert options and prices, a kit for advertisers can be produced. Your advertising kit should be available online as a download and in print format to approach offline businesses. The presentation should include details such as company information, demographics and statistics, advertisement options, and rates and payment methods. Don't forget to run incentives for block-bookings. Convince your potential advertisers that their advert on your site is a good investment.

Sell the benefits:

◆ advertising online is cost-effective

◆ advertisers can monitor results

◆ businesses can reach a targeted audience anywhere in the world.

Tracking statistics for the pay-per-click advertiser

Technology needs to be in place to monitor advertising results, especially if it is a pay-per-click campaign. This statistical information will enable the advertiser to monitor how effective the advert is and will also help them decide whether to continue advertising with you in the future.

If you are offering pay-per-click adverts, you will need ad serving technology to administer this option. This will accurately track results and provide the required statistics for your advertisers. Performance reports are vital if you want to retain your advertisers so ensure that you have this set up if pay-per-click is an option. Even if you're simply running basic advertising on your website, your advertisers will still appreciate traffic reports.

Finding advertisers

Once you have everything in place to start carrying advertising on your website, you need to find your potential advertisers and make them aware of your service.

To attract advertisers, your site has to be one that people talk about. Your web presence needs to be attractive, informative, entertaining, streamlined and of benefit to the visitor with rich content and incentives. Apart from a targeted audience and a large amount of traffic, you also need to prove your establishment, your commitment and site growth potential so that your prospective advertisers will positively benefit from their investment and association with you.

Do the following:

◆ Have an 'Advertise With Us' page on your website together with your advertising kit which should be available as a download.

◆ Place your advertising key words in the meta-tags of the relevant html page and then submit to search engines.

◆ Check out the advertisers on competitors' pages and see if you can offer them a better deal.

◆ Contact offline businesses with your media presentation.

◆ Register with media buyers (see the Resources section).

◆ Try an advertising agency. If you are lacking in time or resources you can outsource this work.

A worthwhile extra income can be earned from advertising, but you need to keep working at it to maintain the right balance.

◆ Keep an eye on current advertising trends as e-commerce changes rapidly as new technology evolves.

◆ Listen to your prospective advertisers. Know what they want and work out what you can offer to provide maximum results.

◆ You need to have a site that is valued by your advertisers so that it attracts more advertisers.

◆ Once space is in demand, you can command a much higher price.

REVIEW YOUR DEVELOPMENT PLAN

Your development plan needs constant attention. Situations change and, when they do, they change rapidly when running an online venture. Review your development plan on a regular basis to make sure that it remains current and applicable. Check your cash flow forecast and web traffic. Ensure that the figures are still in line with your predictions. Revise where necessary and gauge how the results will affect your longer term plans.

DO YOU NEED STAFF?

At some point in your website's growth, you may need to consider recruiting staff. It all depends upon the type of website that you operate. If you sell physical products it's likely that your business may need to consider taking on staff devoted to customer services, after sales support, stock control and processing orders. Even service-based websites may need extra staff, especially if your customer queries start increasing.

There's only so much that a sole trader can do in a day; if the website is suddenly inundated with orders, how would you cope? Would you be able to provide the high level of customer service that your website promises? Of course, this should be considered in your development plan.

If you intend to recruit staff, understand the employers' rules and requirements pertaining to your country. You will need to know your legal obligations concerning health and safety; payment and taxation; and liability insurance. Taking on staff places your business on to another level and your commitments and responsibilities will increase.

If you run a service industry you may be able to hire or commission people to work for you on a freelance/self-employed basis. Again, familiarise yourself with the rules concerning contracts. See the Resources section for links to further information.

DO YOU NEED PREMISES?

Most websites promoting a service can be run from a home office indefinitely. If, however, you sell products, as your business grows it's likely that you'll need larger premises to house your stock.

Many product-based businesses that do well on the internet end up having to move out of their spare room or garage because of lack of space and also because of the need to employ staff. Moving to commercial premises is a big decision though and you will need to review your cash-flow forecast and expenditure plan accordingly.

First take a look at what premises are available. Your local business advice centre should be able to help.

Take into consideration the following points.

◆ Consider whether you are in a position to purchase or rent commercial premises.

◆ Decide what size of premises you need and which will cope with any projected growth.

◆ Gain information on all the running costs involved. This will include business rates, service charges, utility rates, phone and internet services, security and insurance. You will also have costs of setting up the premises with furniture, signage and equipment.

◆ Choose a secure business location which is ideal in terms of travel and access to services that you need.

◆ Estimate the time it will take to move your business and how this will affect the running of your business up to and during the move.

Plan for every possibility and you will minimize the risk of failure.
Remember, everything changes quickly where the internet is concerned.
You need to be ready for action!

Web venture ideas

♦ If you're interested in business and property or have experience in this sector, consider setting up a business sales agency providing online listings of businesses and business property wanted or for sale. You could offer a general service or focus on a niche area such as retail. You would make revenue from those advertising on your site.

CHECKLIST

♦ Plan for growth.

♦ Are you ready if there's a sudden upturn in business?

♦ Do you need staff?

♦ Can you keep your business running effectively if you move premises?

♦ Can you roll out an advertising programme to generate more income for your site?

♦ Do you have contingency plans in place if there are any threats to your website's continuation?

♦ Have you reviewed your development plan?

CASE STUDIES

Darren has an online office supplies business

Darren's online office supplies business has grown considerably since its conception. He has run the venture from an outbuilding at home, but with current development, he's aware that he will outgrow the premises within six months. He needs to find new premises and staff.

Fortunately, Darren planned for growth and has already worked out the next step. He is meeting with a business adviser to talk through the action plan. He has identified suitable premises and can set up and take on two new members of staff within a time frame that won't disrupt existing business. It is still a tentative time though and Darren has considered a contingency plan just in case there are any unforeseen problems.

Jason has developed a business forum online

Jason's successful business forum has consistently high traffic and an opt-in email list of over 40,000. Although he doesn't need premises as the venture is manageable from home, he needs staff to moderate the forums. He decides to take on two freelance website moderators who will work from their own homes. They will be paid per hour for each completed shift. With the growth of the website forum, he has received interest from prospective advertisers and, on sending out his advertising kit, he is confident that he can secure considerable income for the website over the next 12 months.

11
Make More Profit Online

Your web venture may already have enough potential to generate a reasonable income on its own, but it doesn't have to stop there. There are plenty of income generation schemes on the internet which you may be able to explore independently or as an add-on to your existing website. This final chapter looks at the varied opportunities available to make more profit online.

FINDING THE MONEY-MAKERS

As long as the internet evolves there will be someone trying to profit from it. And providing the money-making schemes are legal, authentic and aren't in any way destructive, demeaning or at odds with the spirit of the internet's world wide community, then making a profit online should be encouraged.

My own web developments aside, I've been fortunate to know and work with a number of people who have and still are profiting from internet-based opportunities. Over the years I've witnessed a number of potential opportunities come and go, and I have certainly tried out a few, but there are several that have evolved and offer potential for income generation.

The following suggestions have been tried with varying degrees of success by people I know and are certainly worth exploring. As always though, proceed with care. Do your own independent research on any opportunities you decide to explore. What has worked for one doesn't automatically work for another; but, as ever, with the right approach, you could generate additional income over the short or long term.

START AN AFFILIATE MARKETING BUSINESS

Many people decide to start an online affiliate marketing business because it's quick, easy and profitable. Take a look at the benefits.

◆ You don't have to create a product.

◆ You don't have to worry about providing customer support.

◆ You don't deal with the shipping, returns or any other hassles that come with running a standard sales business.

◆ Affiliate programmes are usually free to join, so you don't have any start-up costs.

◆ You make good profit on sales!

Sounds fantastic! And it can be, with the right approach.

You can promote affiliate products using your own website or the merchant's website. You can even use both options because both methods work; they just work differently for different people. Some affiliates find it easier to have their own website to promote from. Others feel creating a website is too much work, and they find it easier to simply advertise the affiliate product, and let the merchant's website do the selling.

Let's look at the options.

Promoting affiliate products without a website

This can often be the fastest way to start making money with affiliate programmes, but it requires skill, persistence, patience and money. Generally, you would have to pay for advertising to promote the affiliate products. You might use a pay-per-click service such as Google AdWords, and create ads which promote a specific affiliate product. You place the affiliate link with your affiliate code in the ad, and when somebody clicks the ad, the visitor is sent direct to the merchant's website. If the visitor chooses to buy the product, you will be credited with the sale and earn a commission.

Affiliates who use these direct promotional methods to earn money from affiliate products spend their time researching keywords for the most beneficial placement of their ads, and are constantly writing or refining their advertisements for the best results. Most affiliates who use these methods tend to have multiple campaigns going at once. And some of those might make great money while others fail miserably. With time, attention, patience, experience and a reasonable marketing budget, this can turn out to be a lucrative way to make money.

Promoting affiliate products with a website

Here are four popular ways to create affiliate websites.

1. **One-page sales letter, or pre-sell.** This is fairly easy to create, but it helps if you've actually bought the product you intend to promote. By creating just one single page for your website, you keep visitors focused on taking just one action: buying this product. The purpose of a one-page site is to make sure your visitor doesn't become distracted with other ads or content. You want them to buy what you're promoting.

This type of site usually has a detailed product review, or a pre-sell. In general a pre-sell is much like a detailed review. It tends to be 1,000 words or longer, and it explains what you like about a given product. This kind of affiliate marketing site works very well, but it doesn't gain much in the way of organic search engine traffic so most affiliates use pay-per-click advertising or article marketing to send traffic to it.

2. **One-page multi product site.** This is similar to the above, but the main difference is you're comparing multiple products. Generally you should have three to five products on the page, though some affiliate marketers do well comparing as many as ten. It's probably best to keep each page at just three products, so that it doesn't overwhelm your visitors.

With this type of affiliate site you want to create brief product reviews and recommendations. You also want to compare similar products, so the visitor is not pulled in too many directions at once. You also don't want them to be distracted by other elements, so you wouldn't put article content on the site. Just place three to five products with affiliate links for each.

3. **A shopping style e-commerce site.** Many new affiliates don't know you can do this, but it's actually fairly easy to create a fully-fledged e-commerce style shopping site with affiliate products. Some sites have just ten or 20 products on them, but some have 10,000 or more. These types of sites are usually created using an affiliate data-feed and specialised software.

4. **An informational, publication style website.** This type of site usually tends to grow quite large, and it's filled with information. Commonly you'll see sites built with articles on specific topics, and the whole purpose of creating these types of sites is to help bring in natural organic search engine traffic, and gain links from other websites that will send free traffic.

By drawing in targeted traffic to the articles, reports and related content, the webmaster is obtaining visitors on specific topics. They then either recommend certain online merchants and stores, or they list those merchants and stores as related links. With either format the links are of course affiliate links.

Finding good affiliate programmes

When you decide to become an affiliate marketer, the first choice you have to make is what products you'll promote. Hopefully you've already researched and found a lucrative market to target, so now you just need to choose good affiliate products, programmes, and merchants that fit into your overall niche.

It can be a difficult trial and error process for a while, but it doesn't have to be. Here are several key points to consider when looking at affiliate programmes to promote.

1. What's the commission you'll be paid? This tends to be the first thing new affiliates look at, because they want to know how much money they can make with each sale. And most people choose to promote products that offer very high commission rates.

But don't decide on products based solely on the commission percentage amounts. Think about the actual amount of money you'll make instead: 20% of £100 (£20) is much better than 50% of £25 (£12.50).

2. The next important factor to consider is conversion ratio. If you send 100 targeted visitors to an affiliate sales page, how many of those visitors will actually pull out their credit card and buy?

In this instance, percentages count a lot. If 1% of people buy, that's a 1% conversion ratio. That means one person out of 100 will buy on average. If, however, a product has a 10% conversion ratio, then ten people out of 100 will buy.

If you combine conversion ratios with commission rates, you can gain further insight on which product might be the best to promote. Let's say the 50% commission product has a 5% conversion ratio, and the 20% product has a 2% conversion ratio, which product is now the best one to promote? In this case the 50% product is best: from 100 visitors you will earn £62.50 (£12.50 x 5 sales), compared with £40 (£20 x 2 sales) for the 20% product.

No matter how much money a product can earn you, it's worthless if people won't buy it.

3. Look at the sales page itself. This is a step many new affiliate marketers miss. Put yourself in the shoes of the customer. If you were a prospective customer would you buy products or services from this merchant? Is the site easy to use? Is the offer compelling? Is the site professional? Only promote if you can answer yes to all these questions.

Also avoid any merchant who promotes Google AdSense or other affiliate links on their site. Why? Because the site is unfocused and you could end up sending visitors who click on the AdSense ads or affiliate links to their sites and make them money while leaving you out in the cold.

Another problem can sometimes crop up with merchants who sell physical products. It's not uncommon to find a phone number on the sales pages. Often this is a toll free number. The merchant needs to have a contact number, but if they make the number large and prominent, chances are the potential customer you sent to the page will just pick up the phone and bypass you altogether. Some merchants handle this issue well though, and they put a referral code next to their phone number, then they ask for that code when the prospective customer calls (this referral number tracks back to you so that you still earn commission from the sales).

4. What are the merchant's terms? Some merchants put sneaky exception clauses into their terms of service, and affiliates don't realise they won't be paid for various types of sales. Some, for instance, might say affiliates can only earn commission on X items, but not any others. And sometimes they'll even say that affiliates can only earn commission on products under a certain value. So make sure you read the terms and conditions carefully.

5. What are the payout terms? Again, check the terms and conditions. Some merchants will only send commission to you every three months. Some will not pay you until you've generated £100 in commissions. And some will not pay you unless you first generate a certain amount of money, then wait a certain amount of time, then request the payment.

There are many more things to pay attention to when selecting good affiliate programmes, but these are the most important. In general though, do your research. Find out exactly how the programme works and if possible, find out how other affiliates feel about it before committing too much time or money to it yourself.

Affiliate networks

When you get started with affiliate marketing you may not know about affiliate networks. In short, an affiliate network is a third party system that has many different affiliate merchants, products and services all rolled into one.

An affiliate marketer, for instance, can sign up to an affiliate network just once, but choose from hundreds or thousands of merchants to promote. Without using a network, the affiliate would have to sign up at many different sites – one for each merchant or programme they want to promote.

Using an affiliate network usually makes it easier to create links on your websites too. Instead of having to log into many different places to obtain advertising links, pictures or copy . . . you simply log into the network and the links all use the same format.

Often using an affiliate network means you can be paid more often too. If you're promoting ten different merchants individually, and each of those merchants has a minimum earnings requirement before you'll receive payment, it can take much longer to generate enough sales for each one. Using an affiliate network though, all the sales you make for all your merchants are totalled together, so your commission payments are aggregated and you're able to be paid sooner regardless of how many merchants you promote.

This is one of the best reasons to use an affiliate network. Earning £40 each with ten different merchants individually is great . . . but not when it comes to being paid. If each of those merchants requires you to earn at least say £50 before you can have your money, you end up having £400 you can't yet touch.

There are several very good, long-standing, reputable affiliate networks that pay on time all the time, and they combine all your earnings into one cheque. Here's a brief overview of each.

1. Affiliate Window – established in 2000, Affiliate Window works with more UK merchants than any other network. To be paid you have to earn a combined total of £25, and your payment can be directly deposited in your bank account. They pay twice monthly.
www.affiliatewindow.com

2. My Help Hub – this is the central affiliate site for every product in the WCCL Network. They retail dozens of exciting e-books, software tools, and audio CDs. They have no minimum payment requirements and there's no waiting for monthly cheques to clear. They pay after just 35 days – instantly via PayPal for every affiliate sale you make.
www.myhelphub.com

3. Commission Junction – this one has been around the longest, and they have the most merchants to choose from. To be paid you just have to earn a combined total of £25, and you can choose to have your payments directly deposited in your bank account. They pay once a month.
www.cj.com

4. Share A Sale – this affiliate network has been around for several years and it's getting better all the time. They don't have as many merchants as Commission Junction, but they do offer quality merchants and products. To be paid you have to earn a combined total of $50. They can directly deposit your payments in your bank account. They pay once a month.
www.shareasale.com

5. ClickBank – this one has been around for many years and has hundreds of products you can promote. ClickBank only has virtual products: e-books primarily, and some software. They pay every two weeks: the 1st and the 15th.
www.clickbank.com

Affiliate cash flow

Cash flow can be the biggest problem for many new affiliate marketers. Anyone who has run any kind of 'standard' business before understands the concept of cash flow. The same applies if you've run a service based business too. In the case of service businesses, you do the work then send an invoice to your client. Then you wait. Sometimes you wait a long while before that invoice is paid.

With sales based product businesses you buy inventory, or pay rent on your store if it's a physical location, then you try to sell the products you've bought. There are days you might make £200 in sales and days where you make nothing. If, however, you spent £1,000 on inventory or rent . . . you're still in a negative cash flow status even on the day you made £200 in sales.

If you have an offline store you must ask yourself: do you have cash to cover all your expenses until the current inventory reaches break-even? If you're a service based business, you must ask yourself if you have cash to cover regular bills and expenses until invoices are paid.

If you're an affiliate based business, it works similarly to a service based business. Do you have enough cash to cover regular bills and expenses until your affiliate payments arrive?

Lack of cash flow can break a business before it even has a chance to become established. If you spend the last of your available money to advertise, for instance, it doesn't matter how many sales you make or how fast you make them. By spending the last of your money to promote affiliate products and services, you've made yourself broke for an extended period of time.

Affiliate cash flow scheduling issues

Most affiliate programmes pay once each month. And there's a delay built in as well, so it ends up being close to two months before you actually receive your earnings in useable form. Affiliate networks such as Commission Junction and Share a Sale, for instance, pay each month on the 20th. So if you were to make £1,000 in sales on 1 January, you would not actually receive that money until 20 February.

Now there are affiliate programmes and networks that pay every two weeks instead, and this can make cash flow issues less of a problem. But there's still a delay built in. ClickBank, for instance, will send you a cheque on the 1st and 15th of each month, assuming you've earned enough to meet the minimum balance requirements. If that cheque takes three to five days to reach you and then you have to wait for it to clear in your bank, it ends up being closer to three weeks before the money is actually accessible to you.

This scheduling issue is not as problematic once you've become more established, and you're earning commissions on a regular basis. It is important in the beginning though, because that's when cash is needed the most. You're promoting affiliate programmes so that you can make some money, but you must be sure you have enough to survive on until you actually receive the money you've earned.

Residual affiliate programmes

Have you heard the term residual, or recurring affiliate programme, and wondered what it meant? It could quite possibly become your favourite type of affiliate programme to promote. Why? Because with residual affiliate programmes, you can make a sale once, but continue getting paid for that sale over and over again.

A residual affiliate programme is one that pays you multiple times for one sale. Usually you need to promote a service, or a consumable product such as vitamins. And as long as the customer you referred keeps the service, or keeps buying refills on their vitamins regularly, you keep receiving paid commission.

As you can imagine, the cumulative earnings for this type of affiliate marketing can be big. Things can start out slow in the beginning, but over time it adds up very nicely.

Let's look at an example. Let's say you choose to become an affiliate for website hosting services which offer residual payments. So you start promoting those hosting services in whatever ways you choose, just as you would with any other affiliate programme. Using pay-per-click marketing, general websites, articles or otherwise, you start sending targeted traffic to your hosting company affiliate.

Now let's say someone decides to buy a hosting package through your link. As with any other affiliate programme, you earn a commission from that sale. But here's the beauty of residual programmes: If that new customer pays their hosting bill next month, you are paid again. And if they pay again the month after that, you receive another commission and so on.

If that customer stays with the same hosting company for two years, you'll keep being paid every month for two years. If you earn £10 every month, that's £240 you have earned from just one affiliate sale.

Now what if you do that with ten customers? Even better . . . how about generating ten new customers every single month? That's where the true power – and massive income – is made with residual affiliate programmes. It's like having compounded interest on an investment. Ten affiliate sales at £10 each is £100 a month. Add ten new customers each month and because you're also being paid for customers who signed up in previous months, your income is drastically increased without you having to make more sales. In six months you've gained a total of 60 new customers, and you're making £600 a month instead of £100.

Attrition

Now as wonderful as this all sounds, there is a new term you'll become acquainted with and you'll have to factor it into your overall affiliate promotions: attrition. As long as the customer keeps paying for the service you referred them to, you'll continue earning money from them. A certain percentage of customers will stop a service or product in time though, and this is referred to as the attrition rate.

Many web based membership sites, for instance, average only three months per customer. So you'll need to pay attention to the attrition rate of any residual affiliate programme you choose to promote. If it costs a lot of money to acquire a new customer, and you can only count on them staying as a paying customer for three months, you'll need to do some maths. Are you spending more to acquire them than you are making in the three months before they cancel?

Some services retain their customers for years, and when this is the case you can safely spend a fair amount to gain the affiliate sale because you know you'll make much more than that over the entire time they remain a customer.

PROFIT FROM E-PUBLISHING

E-books are electronic versions of books which can be purchased and downloaded online and saved to your desktop or handheld device to either print out or read on screen. Although some believe that e-books will never be as popular as printed books, it's a fact that e-books do sell and can make a healthy profit with the right approach.

You can make a profit online by selling e-books on your website or through other websites via an affiliate scheme.

Consider the advantages of e-books and you'll understand why e-book publishing is appealing.

◆ E-books are cost-effective to produce and distribute.

◆ They are usually instantly available to download and read after purchase.

◆ They can be interactive with clickable links and even animated content.

◆ They are easy to store.

◆ There are no printing costs.

◆ E-books are easy to revise with fresh information. They are ideal for yearbooks or any books that require regular updating.

◆ You can reach a worldwide audience.

◆ E-books tend to have much higher profit margins than their printed contemporaries.

◆ Run an online e-bookstore with automatic payment and download system in place and you can earn even while you sleep!

The best way to profit from e-books, if you have the relevant expertise, is by writing and producing them yourself. E-books that tend to be in demand and generating their good income include the following:

◆ Yearbooks – especially those featuring online reference information.

◆ Special reports from experts.

◆ Specific 'how to' type books which have a niche appeal and aren't widely available in print format.

◆ Success story e-books . . . for example *My Dieting Secrets* or *How I Made My First Million*.

◆ E-books that provide solutions to problems.

The more useful the information, the more e-books you'll sell! Some e-books command a much higher retail price than printed books and this is especially the case with quality information or books revealing secrets. Special reports can command triple figures! Not bad when you consider that the costs per e-book are negligible.

E-book publishing tips

◆ Write an e-book that has a definite market. It will help you focus your marketing efforts.

◆ Consider your sales page for your e-book. Commission a copywriter to do the page justice.

◆ Think about your e-book's title. Capture the attention of your readers. Your title needs to have impact: *Discover the Truth About . . .* or *How to be Successful at . . . Profit from . . . The Secrets of . . .* , etc.

◆ Write to suit a worldwide audience. Read the earlier section on writing web content as the same rules basically apply.

◆ It's often more profitable to sell your e-books from your own website, but experiment to see what works best for you.

◆ If there is good profit in your e-book, set up an affiliate scheme. This will increase your marketing efforts considerably and also enhance your profits.

How to create your e-books

Most e-books are written in MS Word, or other text or page design program, then presented into a PDF which is formatted ready for purchase and download. There are plenty of e-book programs available which provide simple solutions as well as help you produce a more complex e-book with interactive features if required.

If you simply want to write e-books and let someone else take care of publishing, there are plenty of e-book publishers on the internet. Check out the Resources section for details.

MAKING INCOME FROM INFORMATION

Personal pages aside, the internet has millions of information portals throughout the world, all vying for attention. Information is what makes the net desirable, but unless you can gain revenue from the provision of information, maintaining a profitable website can prove challenging.

Major information portals such as Yahoo and MSN gain revenue from advertising and selling other services. Community information portals, especially, have had to evolve rapidly over the years under financial pressures. Yet, smaller and more niche information websites are being established all the time. So how do they make their income?

Most are set up to gain revenue from two main sources. They use either Google.com Adsense or a range of targeted affiliate programmes. The idea is to use the information website to attract high volumes of traffic in the hope that a reasonable percentage will click through the adverts onsite or make purchases through the targeted affiliate ads. An information website that has been optimised can generate a few hundred pounds per month – more in some cases! All you have to do is occasionally place new content on the website to maintain interest and keep the site current while actively marketing it. It should take you a few hours a week to maintain the site. If you have a website that is related to a high key word/term result, you could make some nice additional income from little effort.

Tips

◆ Start by doing a key word search to see how popular the key terms relating to your chosen subject area are in the search engines.

◆ If possible, draw upon existing interests or expertise. It will be easier to create a popular, informative website that people will want to visit.

◆ Place your ad campaigns in prominent positions on each information web page. A column on either the left or right or across the top of your web page enhances visibility.

- ◆ Choose suitable affiliates relating to your subject area and which have a reasonable commission rate.

- ◆ Use a variety of marketing tactics to drive visitors to the website.

BID FOR BUSINESS

If you offer a service the internet is a fantastic resource for finding clients and contracts. Over the years a number of thriving 'bid for business' websites have appeared and remained on the scene, drawing in buyers and sellers in the business-to-business (B2B) service industry.

For the freelance looking to secure more income online, the scope for securing work using the bidding system is good. Bid for business schemes often provide many one-off commissions on a work for hire contract, but if the business-to-business relationship is an agreeable one, then there is scope for ongoing work.

For the company searching for a service provider, the internet is the perfect arena where buyers and sellers can meet up and conduct business. By sending their project to auction, it presents them with a wider choice of candidates for the job, making remote outsourcing viable.

Bid-for-business is ideal for service providers such as: writers, artists, photographers, web designers, computer programmers, accountants, book-keepers, editors, proof-readers, tutors, consultants, astrologers, designers, business advisers, translators, researchers and data entry contractors.

How it works

The concept of having to bid for work constructively challenges the way the work place does business. Projects are posted on the bid-for-work website and then you simply place bids to try to win the work being offered. You may be thinking that it sounds like an auction – a little like bidding for something on eBay. Without a doubt, it is competitive but your success at winning contracts depends upon a number of factors. These include your ability, area of expertise, price of bid (although not always considered important) and the way in which you present yourself.

The scheme is relatively easy to use. Your bid and proposal will be posted on the site along with your competitors'. You can bid for any number of projects posted on a daily basis while also advertising yourself on a site's database which companies can access. Often, this can bring in extra opportunities from companies requiring a specific service. This certainly provides scope for the specialist service provider!

There are a number of established business-to-business bid-for-work market places that you can register with. Some sites charge commissions for successful bids completed while others just charge the companies looking for service providers. Check the small print before you sign up to any sites and make sure you're happy with the terms.

Advantages:

◆ The bid-for-work service provides access to a wide range of potential contracts in your area of expertise.

◆ You can display your online portfolio on the bid-for-business website so that you are visible to your potential clients.

◆ Once registered, you will have access to other facilities such as shared work-space, file sharing, international billing and project management.

Disadvantages:

◆ Some may find the prospect of bidding for work intimidating.

◆ You tend to have to compete with low bids.

◆ It is highly competitive.

◆ You can't afford to make mistakes when providing your service as the client can leave feedback on the site.

Writing a successful bid

Once you register with a bid-for-business website, work on presenting a winning bid that will entice the company to hire you.

Follow these guidelines to help you place a successful bid.

◆ Read the project description thoroughly.

◆ Only bid for projects that you can realistically deliver. There's nothing worse than bidding for work and then letting a company down.

◆ Before you post your bid, weigh up competitors' bids and proposals. Will your bid be competitive?

◆ Write a brief but informative profile bid, highlighting the strengths you can bring to the project.

◆ Provide a link to your resumé and samples of work.

◆ Thoroughly check your proposal and resumé, to make sure there are no mistakes. Is your resumé up to date?

◆ Make sure you will be able to deliver the work to the required deadline.

◆ Be professional in your approach. Your bid (unless a hidden bid), resumé and project proposal will be open to public view.

Tips for securing bid-for-work contracts

To secure bid-for-work contracts, consider the following:

◆ Be confident in your presentation. Your portfolio, bio and pitch are visible to all who use the site (including competitors).

◆ Highlight any areas of speciality and expertise when placing your bids.

◆ List any relevant experience working for similar companies.

◆ Be flexible and negotiable in your terms and working arrangement.

◆ Provide endorsements provided by previously satisfied clients.

◆ Register with a variety of online business-to-business market places.

◆ Check the websites on a daily basis for new postings.

◆ Check out your competitors first and consider what additional benefits you can provide to the client.

◆ Make sure that your resumé/business profile and samples of your work are up to date and available on each site for companies to access.

◆ Remember that companies won't necessarily take the lowest bid. They will opt for your expertise, quality and reliability so don't be afraid of giving a higher bid.

Bid-for-Business online is certainly innovative in bringing together clients and service providers. I have used it myself and won a number of projects in the past. Good working relationships can be forged along the way. If you are a service provider looking to make extra income online as well as securing remote working contracts, then the bid-for-business approach is worth checking out.

Web venture ideas

◆ Are you good at woodwork, crafts, making designer wear or creating ceramics? Can you turn your hobby into a classy craft website selling one-off designer pieces? Although handmade crafts are time consuming, you can command a higher price for one-off pieces. You can also be open to accepting commissions. Look to the skills you have. The web provides potential for talented individuals.

EXPLORE DROP SHIPPING

Drop shipping is where a wholesale distributor will ship their products for you. You market and sell a product online from your own website or online auction site at a price you choose. After your customer purchases the item, you place an order for the product you have just sold with the drop shipper. The drop shipper charges you a wholesale price and ships the product direct to your customer. You make your profit on the difference between the wholesale and retail prices.

The best part about drop shipping is that you do not have to carry or finance any stock, and you don't have to negotiate the logistics of shipping. This is ideal if you're looking for a relatively low-risk and low-cost way of making some additional income via the internet. But do your homework; while there are many legitimate opportunities, there are just as many scams.

What to look for

If you're interested, consider the following pointers when looking for a product line and a reputable drop shipping company to work with.

◆ First, you must find a product that will sell in big enough numbers and at a sufficient mark-up to make it profitable and worthwhile.

◆ Research the market for any product line that you are considering. You need to find how big the demand is for the product and how much competition there is, and what the competition is charging.

◆ Focus on listening to the market and discovering the products your visitors want to buy.

◆ Check out a variety of drop shipping companies. Find out what reputation they have. Look for recent testimonials.

◆ Find out how long the drop shippers have been around for. Young drop ship companies and wholesalers have the habit of going bust quickly, or growing too rapidly, and as a consequence basic good customer service suffers.

◆ You can contact wholesale suppliers of products you wish to sell and ask them if they operate a drop shipping programme, and then open an account with the company.

◆ It's best to start off with selling only a few products, or at least products that are related and targeted at the same market. This will help you concentrate your marketing efforts where they will make the most impact.

◆ Watch out for those scams! Check out the scam lists of drop shippers. Take care that you're not dealing with middlemen posing as drop shippers who will charge you more than you need to pay.

◆ It's important to know all the costs involved so you can calculate your profit margins accurately. Any wholesale company that wants to charge you a regular 'participation' fee should be avoided – the only time you should have to pay a drop shipping company anything is in connection with a specific order.

Avoiding difficulties

Although some of the hassles of online business are eliminated with drop shipping, not all of them are. There will be times when the product you've just sold is out of stock at your suppliers. There will also be returns and refunds to deal with. Work these issues through with your drop shipper ahead of time, so you'll know how to deal with them when they arise.

The last thing you want is to be caught up in a nasty situation where you have a number of returns – and have to foot the bill. Ask the drop shipping company about their returns policy and about any guarantees associated with their products. Make sure you have the terms and conditions in writing and that you understand the small print. Remember, it's your reputation on the line.

If you find a reputable drop shipper to work with and a product with a healthy profit margin, there's potential to do reasonably well with the right marketing efforts. However, the mark-up on most products can be quite low. You would need to sell a lot to make a huge difference and your success depends upon how many other drop shippers are selling the same product line.

Ultimately, if you want more control and the best prices, you really need to be looking at buying your own stock in bulk and up front. Then you're entering a whole new experience as an e-tailer (online retailer)!

SELLING ON EBAY

eBay is rated as the world's biggest online auction website. With phenomenal levels of traffic and trading, it's not surprising that this internet giant provides a starting place for online traders.

Most people start by buying a few things on eBay and then selling some items they already have lying around the house. This not only helps you clear some space, but also puts some money in your pocket. It also helps you learn the basics of eBaying and gives your account a positive feedback score.

From this start you can steadily grow a serious business on eBay. Generally, you can sell almost anything (though observe the list of things you can't sell) from string and cardboard boxes through to cars, houses and even aeroplanes! The secret to success is being able to sell popular products with excellent profit margins which will allow you to sell at a discount and still make a decent mark-up.

Let's look at some key strategies you can use to build your business into an eBay success story.

1. Be specific

Use a well-worded title to drive traffic to your listings. The key to attracting targeted eBay buyers to your listing is to make your listing title as specific as possible. That way, your list will attract people who are looking for the exact item you're selling. A good title is by far the most important part of your auction.

When potential buyers search for items on eBay, the title is the first thing they see. Depending on what you're selling, some searches can bring up hundreds of results. With so many competitors, it's vital that your title captures your potential buyers' attention and encourages them to click through to your item and not somebody else's.

To optimise your title and drive traffic to your listings remember to include the item name and brand name in your listing title and use descriptive words. Keep it short and to the point. And make sure you spell-check your title; misspellings decrease the amount of traffic an auction receives.

2. Avoid reserve pricing

Never use reserve pricing; most buyers find reserve auctions frustrating. The best thing to do is set your opening bid as the lowest amount you'll accept for the item.

By taking into account the price you paid for the item, and working out how much the item will cost in eBay fees, you will know exactly what price to start the auction so you at least make a small profit.

3. Buy It Now

Many eBay PowerSellers choose to list Buy It Now using the fixed price format, where you simply indicate the price at which you'd like to sell your items. Buyers can purchase from your listings immediately at that price. To determine at what price to set your Buy It Now item look at your sales history to see what price the same or similar items have sold for in the past. If it's an item you haven't listed before, check to see what other sellers have sold it for by using eBay's Advanced Search for Completed Listings Only.

Items with no sales history can be set at full retail price, but on eBay you would be very lucky to achieve this! Most items on eBay are set at 30% or more below retail. Just make sure you are making at least 40% mark-up on the trade price you paid (if you paid £5 for an item you will want to sell it for at least £7) or it's just not worth your time to stock that item. You want to be aiming for 100% or more mark-up.

4. Selling multiples

If you're selling multiples of an item, space them out, rather than selling them all at once. That's simply supply and demand at work. You don't want to flood the market.

5. Using photos

Use photos in your listings. This one is obvious, but so many sellers still list items without a photo. Most people just won't bid on an item that doesn't have at least one photo. Generally speaking, you will obtain more active bidders the better your photos are, and the more bidders competing for your item, the higher the sale price.

6. Describing the item

Give a complete description of your item, including any and all flaws. The more descriptive your auction is, the more comfortable you'll make the buyer feel. They'll know exactly what they're gaining and won't have any unexpected surprises once they receive the item. Therefore you won't receive any unwanted negative feedback.

Use fun stories when describing your item. This tends to stimulate extra interest in the item. Also if you're selling the item well below the retail price, state this in the description. Research has shown that auctions that mention the high retail price sell for 7% more on average.

7. Shipping charges

Some eBay sellers pump up their shipping charges to generate a few extra pounds in profit, but beware! Overcharging on shipping can damage your credibility. Inflated shipping can potentially cost you the sale if a buyer chooses to deal with another seller who charges less for sending the same item. Make your profits on the actual sale of your item and you will build your credibility and positive feedback in the process.

Feedback scores

Avoid negative feedback. Sellers who have high positive feedback scores are much more likely to have their auctions result in a sale. Positively rated sellers also receive higher bids.

SELLING YOUR BUSINESS

Assuming that you take the route of setting up a web venture and have built it into a profitable online empire, you can carry on and reap the rewards, or you could sell your web venture. Selling could prove to be an exciting and lucrative deal, especially if your website has a substantial and growing flow of traffic or a healthy sales record.

Websites are being bought and sold daily. As is the case with offline businesses, there are always entrepreneurs looking for a ready-made online venture that they can purchase, ranging from small sole-trader websites to large e-commerce businesses.

Evaluate the reasons why you would sell your online venture. Perhaps you want to:

◆ take early retirement

◆ explore other web ventures or pursuits

◆ spend your time working on a new venture

◆ make a large profit from your web venture to give you funds to invest elsewhere in your life.

To check whether you have a proposition that would be attractive, consider the following:

◆ How much traffic are you generating?

◆ Are you gaining and retaining customers?

◆ Do you have an extensive customer mailing list?

◆ Have your profits grown year-on-year?

◆ Is there scope for more development?

If you have a viable and profitable (or potentially profitable) web venture, you are certainly in an enviable position to sell your business for a decent profit. You will need to gain professional advice to ascertain what your business is worth and to set the process in motion. There are many websites devoted to the sale and purchase of web ventures. Conduct a search and check the resource section for examples.

AVOIDING SCAMS

There are plenty of money-making opportunities on the internet, but you need to be wary of the inevitable scams that masquerade as viable businesses but are actually out to steal your money!

Observe the following golden rules to avoid falling prey to the scam-merchants.

◆ If a venture looks too good to be true, it probably is.

♦ Research the opportunity thoroughly.

♦ Speak to others who have used the system.

♦ Be cautious about parting with your money!

♦ Thoroughly check the credentials of any business. Note how long the company has been established and whether they have a good reputation that can be traced.

♦ Check that the business has a physical address and contact information.

♦ Check to see if the business is connected with a well-known governing body or association that gives them credibility. Don't take their word for it though. Check to see if they are actually on the list.

♦ Search for the latest scams. There are online organisations that expose scams and will provide updates.

♦ Seek professional advice from business, legal or trade associations if you have any doubts.

 The internet is constantly evolving and new profit-making opportunities are being launched all the time. When choosing from the various schemes available, remember the maxim: if it looks too good to be true, it probably is! Do your research. Make sure the figures add up correctly . . . and be careful! Choose recommendations that you can trust.

CONSIDER FINAL TIPS

Reflect on the following:

♦ Do a search for online income generation opportunities. Although there's plenty of rubbish on the net, you may come across some viable propositions.

♦ Remember . . . watch out for those scams! They exist in abundance. The golden rules are: check details and small print of any opportunity; do not part with your money without taking professional advice; research the opportunity thoroughly and try to talk with people who are in the same business area for an overall appraisal.

◆ Keep in touch with developments. New opportunities come online constantly. They aren't always obvious though. You may need to do some lateral thinking on how you can turn a new development into an income generation opportunity.

◆ Consider whether any offbeat or little-known offline business ideas will work online.

◆ Can you collaborate with an inventor or manufacturer to bring a new product into the online market place?

◆ Many great online ventures result from finding answers to everyday problems or targeting a product/service with a niche, international market.

◆ Watch out for market trends. Look to establish a web venture in a growth area. For example, environmentally-friendly products and solutions as well as lifestyle-enhancing products are currently high up on the list in terms of business growth.

◆ Be a good entrepreneur. Run a venture that makes you proud. Provide a service that you would expect for yourself or your family. Be ethical and authentic in your business decisions and share your success with others.

Web venture ideas

◆ It's difficult to come up with an original idea. Most successful web ventures are based upon concepts that have been tried and tested. What makes them different is the slant or approach taken. You could choose a business that has hundreds of competitors. It's what you bring to the venture that will make it successful.

EXPLORING INTERNET BUSINESS IDEAS

Let's end with some suggestions for website ventures. Many of these are (probably) already out there vying for customers in cyberspace; however, it may create a spark for other ideas.

◆ One of the biggest growth areas is in products and services which are eco-friendly or can reduce the impact on the climate. Research and development into this area could have fantastic benefits.

◆ Recycle scrap into artistic sculptures to sell as one-off designer pieces.

◆ Create customised novelty film posters where customers choose to have their name and their friends' names on the poster as the movie's stars.

◆ Create and sell rosettes for country shows.

◆ Sell dolls' house furniture. The items are small to stock and deliver.

◆ Love horses? How about a website dedicated to listing horses for sale and wanted. You earn from advertising revenue.

◆ Interested in music? Sell musical instrument accessories such as guitar strings, plectrums, drum sticks and tuners.

◆ Use your expertise. Deliver an online course; write an e-book; provide free advice and generate income from affiliates and advertising.

◆ Do you run a guest house/hotel? Consider niche holidays such as an artists' weekend or a meditation week and use the website to promote your activities.

◆ Could you make and sell designer bird-boxes or garden ornaments?

◆ Look to provide a solution for a niche audience: shoes for small or big feet; gadgets for people who are left-handed; health products for people who have allergies.

◆ Focus on a single topic – a website for dog owners or a particular dog breed. Sell related pictures, stationery and gift items.

◆ Interested in collectables? There could be scope to run a collectors' club online where you can have a members' only area and collectable items listed for sale.

◆ Start a social community website. We've already seen several become successful ventures. Perhaps you can start one aimed at a particular age group or interest group.

◆ The gift market is huge but people are always looking for something a bit different to give to loved ones. Can you develop a novelty gift in a box? Teddy bears are popular, but can you make them different – miniature guardian angel teddy bears perhaps which your loved ones can take on their travels? It's probably already been done. Look for a different angle.

◆ Lifestyle consultancy has been all the rage. There are coaches to help you live more healthily; to enhance your fitness; to improve your bank balance; to help you downshift; to guide you towards living a more fulfilling life. Is it time for something different? Morbid as it might seem, how about a coaching service that helps you prepare for the end of your earthly life? Or how about a consultancy service for people who wish to make their homes eco-friendly?

◆ Anything wacky, weird and fun always attracts interest or curiosity. The more wacky and fun, the greater number of people will visit your website. People enjoy a little escapism. A chance to eliminate stress and hum-drum daily life remains ever appealing. So, a website that is fun to visit could prove to be a hit. Think about animated cartoon websites; strange customs and conventions; mysteries of the unexplained; virtual reality games.

◆ A website devoted to listing themed holidays in the UK, USA, Europe or around the world such as eco-friendly holidays; unusual or historic holiday properties; spa breaks; farm holidays; island or coastal breaks; canal boat holidays. Generate income from advertising and/or affiliates.

Remember that the success of your internet business rests entirely with you. Create a website to be proud of. Provide a service that is second to none. Offer solutions to satisfy the demand. Run your web venture with a positive, dynamic outlook and believe in what you're doing wholeheartedly.

CASE STUDIES

Sienna sells fashion accessories on eBay

Sienna has a young family and wanted to look for some extra income which used her love of fashion. She researched online trading after finding a good supplier of low cost fashion accessories. Not really interested in setting up her own e-commerce website or developing a major business, she decided to try eBay to sell the popular line of accessories. She started selling a few items a week and this has increased to several items each day. She has set up a store front on eBay to enhance her presence on the website and so that anyone taking part in an auction can look at other accessories in her store and choose to 'Buy It Now'. The part-time venture is manageable and is generating several hundreds of pounds net profit each month.

Ben is a freelance web designer securing work online

Ben used to work as a web designer for a large company, but became tired and disillusioned with the long commute each day. He spent a few months developing a plan to become self-employed as a freelance web designer. Although a competitive field, he felt that with the right approach and consistent marketing he would be able to gain enough work to sustain him.

Ben developed a great website to promote his services and created a few free websites for friends to build his portfolio. He knew that starting out would be tough so he visited numerous freelance websites to pick up opportunities. He tried a bid-for-business website and found a good selection of projects that he felt able to do. He placed a number of bids, not really expecting anything, but was delighted when he won two contracts. He completed the contracts to receive excellent feedback which increased his rating on the bid-for-business site. Since then he has won additional contracts, some of which have led to ongoing design work and recommendations.

CONCLUSION

Despite its occasional tantrums and teething troubles, the internet is evolving into a more reliable and streamlined network, linking people of the world to share information and trading. With enormous leaps in technology taking place almost daily, and the move towards accessible and affordable mobile internet, greater numbers of people over the coming years will venture online to the World Wide Web than ever before.

For you, the budding internet entrepreneur, this is undoubtedly an ideal time to start an online venture. With the right approach you could easily establish yourself as one of tomorrow's big names on the World Wide Web. At the very least, and perhaps more appealing, you can run a web venture that will generate an income that may provide you and your family with extra funds to enjoy the luxuries in life or even enough to start a totally new lifestyle.

Whatever direction you decide, I hope you feel inspired and I wish you and your web venture much success for the future. Switch on your computer and start living your dream!

Carol Anne Strange

Resources

The following section provides a list of website links that you may find useful for gaining further information on topics mentioned.

ADVERTISING ANALYTICS

Microsoft Ad Centre Lab http://adlab.msn.com

AFFILIATE NETWORK

Affiliate Window www.affiliatewindow.com

ClickBank www.clickbank.com

Commission Junction, global leader in online advertising channels and affiliate marketing www.cj.com

myHelpHub.com, the central affiliate site for every product in the WCCL Network www.myhelphub.com/start/menu.aspx?a=affiliatesignup&

Share a Sale www.shareasale.com

AFFILIATE SOFTWARE

Affiliate Wiz www.affiliatewiz.com

ANTI-VIRUS SOFTWARE

Grisoft –AVG www.grisoft.com

McAfee www.mcafee.com

Symantec www.symantec.com

ANTI-VIRUS NEWS

The Register http://www.theregister.co.uk/security/virus/

ARTICLE DIRECTORIES

Ezine Articles www.ezinearticles.com
Go Articles www.goarticles.com
Idea Marketers www.ideamarketers.com

BID-FOR-BUSINESS WEBSITES

Elance.com www.elance.com
SmartHunt.com www.smarthunt.com

BLOGGING

www.blogger.com
www.typepad.com
www.wordpress.com

BUSINESS ADVICE

Business Gateway www.bgateway.com
Business Link www.businesslink.gov.uk
Growing Business for Entrepreneurs www.growingbusiness.co.uk
Small Biz Pod www.smallbizpod.co.uk
Startups.co.uk provides business advice, news and online start-up profiles
www.startups.co.uk
UK Business Forums a great forum for sharing business advice and networking
www.ukbusinessforums.co.uk

COPYRIGHT INFORMATION

Copyright in the UK www.patent.gov.uk
Copyright in the USA www.copyright.gov

CONSUMER ISSUES

Consumer Direct (UK) www.consumerdirect.gov.uk

CONTENT PROVIDERS

WriteThisMoment If you need a writer to provide sales copy, content for your website or e-books, you can advertise your requirements free on this site! www.writethismoment.net

Photography Update If you need a photographer to provide images for your website or product photography, you can advertise your requirements free on this site. www.photographyupdate.com

DATA PROTECTION

Information Commissioners Office UK www.ico.gov.uk

DOMAIN NAMES

Nominet is the internet registry for UK domain names www.nominet.org.uk
Easily.co.uk an established UK domain company http://easily.co.uk/

E-BOOK CREATORS

Adobe www.adobe.com
PDF Creator www.pdf-creator.net

E-BOOK PUBLISHERS

BookLocker.com www.booklocker.com
Lulu.com www.Lulu.com

EMAIL NEWSLETTERS MAILING PROVIDERS

Aweber www.aweber.com
Topica www.liszt.com
Your Mailing List Provider www.yourmailinglistprovider.com
IContact www.icontact.com

EMPLOYMENT LAW

British Employment Law www.emplaw.co.uk
Department of Trade and Industry (UK) www.dti.gov.uk/employment/index.html

EXPERT ADVICE

Expert Sources find experts or be listed as an expert, www.expertsources.co.uk

EZINE DIRECTORY

www.ezine-dir.com
www.go-ezines.com
www.bestezines.com

FREE STUFF

Free articles:

Article City submit articles or obtain articles www.articlecity.com
Get My Articles www.getmyarticles.com
How It Works http://howitworks.net

Free content for your website:

Free Sticky www.freesticky.com/stickyweb

INTELLECTUAL PROPERTY

The UK Patent Office www.patent.gov.uk

INTERNET BUSINESS TOOLS

www.internet-business-tools.com/business

INTERNET INDUSTRY NEWS

Ecommerce Times www.ecommercetimes.com
World Technology News http://worldtechnews.com/

INTERNET RESEARCH

Forrester Research partners with you to create business and technology strategies
www.forrester.co.uk

INTERNET SECURITY

www.getsafeonline.org
www.pcsolutions.co.uk/risk.html

KEYWORD DENSITY TOOL

www.keyworddensity.com
www.seotoolkit.co.uk
www.seochat.com/seo-tools/keyword-density

KEYWORD SELECTOR TOOL

https://adwords.google.com/select/KeywordToolExternal

LEGAL ADVICE

Website-Law.co.uk offers some free legal documents which you can revise for your
own website including terms and conditions, privacy notice and disclaimer
www.website-law.co.uk

MEDIA BUYERS

www.srds.com

PAY-PER-CLICK ADVERTISING

Google.com AdWords Help Centre https://adwords.google.com/support
Microsoft http://advertising.microsoft.com/directresponse
Yahoo Sponsored Search http://searchmarketing.yahoo.com

PRODUCT REVIEWS

Cnet.co.uk http://www.cnet.co.uk/

ONLINE PAYMENT SYSTEMS

Authorize.net www.authorize.net
Nochex www.nochex.com
PayPal www.paypal.com
WorldPay www.worldpay.com

ONLINE TRADING

eBay www.ebay.com

www.cqout.com

SEARCH DIRECTORY

DMOZ open directory project www.dmoz.com

SEARCH ENGINES

Alta Vista www.altavista.com

Google www.google.com

Lycos www.lycos.com

MSN www.msn.com

Yahoo www.yahoo.com

SEARCH ENGINE INFORMATION

http://searchenginewatch.com

www.traffick.com

SEARCH ENGINE MARKETING AND OPTIMISATION

www.searchenginemarketing.org.uk

http://searchmarketing.yahoo.com/

SOFTWARE

Kashflow accounting software www.kashflow.co.uk

Open Source CMS www.opensourcecms.com

Website design software www.xsitepro.com

WEB BUSINESSES FOR SALE

www.webbusinessesforsale.co.uk

www.bizsale.co.uk/index.html

WEB DESIGNERS

Freelancers.net find a web designer for your project www.freelancers.net

WEBMASTER INFORMATION

Site Pro www.sitepronews.com

WEBSITE HOSTING

www.4uhosting.co.uk

www.nativespace.co.uk

SiteSell.com all-in-one build and host package www.sitesell.com

WEBSITE TESTING AND QUALITY ASSURANCE

www.usertesting.com

WEBSITE USABILITY INFORMATION

Usability First www.usabilityfirst.com/index.txl

Webcredible.co.uk www.webcredible.co.uk

Index

Some other titles from How To Books

WORK FROM HOME

Judy Heminsley

Whether you are planning to run your own business or work from home as an employee for a large company, you will share experiences and be looking for solutions to similar challenges. This is a down-to-earth, practical and friendly guide, designed to help you get the best out of working from home. It includes lots of options to help you choose and develop the arrangements that best suit you and your family. In it you'll discover: whether you and your work are suited to working from home; how to negotiate homeworking with your employer; how to maintain a professional image; how to separate work from home; and much more.

ISBN 978-1-84528-335-3

PREPARE TO SELL YOUR COMPANY

L B Buckingham

Selling your company is a trying time, similar to selling your house. For those unfamiliar with this process, the challenging thoughts will be: 'How do I start?'; 'Who can help me?'; 'How much can I get for the business?'; 'Who is most likely to buy it, and where do I find them?'; 'When should I do it?' This book will answer all your questions. Easy to read, it covers all the practical aspects of preparing your business for sale. It will show you just how a potential acquirer will view a company that is up for sale. This will enable you to develop a business profile that will attract buyers – and maintain their interest until completion, and build into the business those aspects that will encourage a buyer to increase their bid. This book will take you through the sale process: preparation, marketing, acceptance of offer, the `due diligence examination' (the vendor's nightmare), successful completion, and beyond.

ISBN 978-1-84528-328-5

The Institute of Certified Bookkeepers

MASTERING BOOK-KEEPING

Dr Peter Marshall

An accredited textbook of The Institute of Chartered Bookkeepers.

This updated 8th edition contains extracts from ICB, AAT, OCR and AQA sample examination papers.

'This book has been planned to cover the requirements of all the major examining boards' syllabuses and achieves all it sets out to do.'
Focus on Business Education

'Presented in a clear and logical manner – written in plain English.'
Learning Resources News

'This book has great potential value.' *Educational Equipment Magazine*

ISBN 978-1-84528-324-7

THE SMALL BUSINESS START-UP WORKBOOK

Cheryl D. Rickman

'I would urge every business adviser in the land to read this book.'
Sylvia Tidy-Harris, Managing Director of www.womenspeakers.co.uk

'Inspirational and practical workbook that takes you from having a business idea to actually having a business. By the time you have worked through the exercises and checklists you will be focussed, confident and raring to go.' www.allthatwomenwant.co.uk

'A real 'must have' for anyone thinking of setting up their own venture.' –
Thames Valley News

'. . . a very comprehensive book, a very readable book.' –
Sister Business E-Zine

ISBN   978-1-84528-038-3

START AND RUN A SANDWICH AND COFFEE BAR
Jill Sutherland

In this step-by-step guide, the owner of a multi-award winning sandwich and coffee bar tells how you, too, can turn your passion for food into a successful business. Jill Sutherland`s comprehensive guide will take you on a stage-by-stage guide to your first year, from idea to opening and then to becoming established. Packed with top tips, real-life examples, checklists and anecdotes, this book provides you with practical and realistic advice from someone who has been there and done it. In it you'll learn how to develop and research your sandwich bar 'idea'; write a professional business plan; find the right shop unit, and fit it out; find and manage suppliers; manage food hygiene, and health and safety; create your menu and source produce; budget, forecast and manage cash flow; launch and generate publicity and employ and manage staff.

ISBN 978-1-84528-333-9

STARTING A BUSINESS FROM HOME
Paul Power

This book will show you how to turn your passion and enthusiasm into a viable business. It is packed full of practical, down-to-earth advice based on the author's own, and other successful entrepreneurs', experience. Discover how you can easily research your ideas, start your own business at home, from little or nothing and market your business on a shoestring. 'His no-nonsense approach is inspirational.' *Goodtimes*

ISBN   978-1-84528-301-8

HOW TO START AND RUN A PETSITTING BUSINESS

Fiona Mckenzie

'An absolutely MUST HAVE for anyone that is starting up their own business. The book covers everything you need to know from a person who has gone through it themselves, and is written in a humourous helpful way. A book you will find essential when you are setting up and also to keep to refer to over the years once your business is up and running.' Reader review

ISBN 978-1-84528-289-9

START & RUN A SUCCESSFUL CLEANING BUSINESS

Robert Gordon

This book will give you insider knowledge of the world of office and domestic cleaning and provide you with all the practical tools you need to succeed in a competitive but rewarding industry.

ISBN 978-1-84528-284-4

HOW TO BUY AND RUN YOUR OWN HOTEL

Mark Lloyd

'Holds your hands as you give up the safety of your current profession and leap into the unknown.' Food & Catering

'Covering all aspects of the process, from the initial set-up, to daily running and even marketing your hotel.' French Magazine

'This book really is essential reading for anyone considering buying and running a hotel.' The Landlord Law Blog

ISBN   978-1-84528-275-2

STARTING & RUNNING A GREETINGS CARD BUSINESS

Elizabeth White

'Tells the reader everything they need to know about building an exciting and profitable business.' Greetings Today

This book takes you step by step through the process of starting and running a business with lots of useful practical advice to help you.

ISBN 978-1-84528-264-6

How To Books are available through all good bookshops, or you can order direct from us through Grantham Book Services.

Tel: +44 (0)1476 541080
Fax: +44 (0)1476 541061

Or Via our website

www.howtobooks.co.uk

To order via any of these methods please quote the title(s) of the book(s) and your credit card number together with its expiry date.

For further information about our books and catalogue, please contact:

How To Books
Spring Hill House
Spring Hill Road
Begbroke
Oxford OX5 1RX

Visit our website at

www.howtobooks.co.uk

Or you can contact us by email at info@howtobooks.co.uk